Dr Michael Nathenson is an American who has been working in England for the past 12 years. He holds two degrees in Social Psychology and a PhD in Education Communications. He is currently a Senior Lecturer in Education at The Open University and the author of two books and numerous articles on educational testing and evaluation.

Doris Long runs a word-processing bureau in North London. She is married and has two children. She was born in California and worked for the United States Foreign Service as Secretary to Ambassadors in Venezuela and Burundi. She also lived in Vietnam for four years. She helped organize the first children's poetry festival in Cambridge and ran school book shops for seven years.

MICHAEL NATHENSON
AND DORIS LONG

London
Without Tears

30 Comprehensive Itineraries
for Parents and Kids

Drawings by Ivor Sexton

GRAFTON BOOKS

A Division of the Collins Publishing Group

LONDON GLASGOW
TORONTO SYDNEY AUCKLAND

Grafton Books
A Division of the Collins Publishing Group
8 Grafton Street, London W1X 3LA

A Grafton Paperback Original 1986

Copyright © Michael Nathenson and Doris Long 1986

ISBN 0-586-06769 8

Printed and bound in Great Britain by
Collins, Glasgow

Set in Century Schoolbook

To Hadley, Ben, Elizabeth,
Zoe and Eli.

A special thanks to Dasha Shenkman for her
support on this book and all the others.

Contents

Introduction

It has been a wonderful experience to visit all the places in this book, gathering together the strands of history and weaving them into a clearer picture of time.

We are sure you will enjoy marvelling at the Crown Jewels, rambling over Hampstead Heath, beating time with the soldiers as they change guard and hearing the voice of Winston Churchill giving encouragement to the people of the British Isles during World War II.

We hope that this book will take all the drudgery out of touring London for you. Unlike all the other tour books for children – which simply list places to see and leave it to you to plan your day – *London Without Tears* offers you an organized day tour, from 10 A.M. to 3 P.M.; more important, each tour focuses on a theme like, for example, a Charles Dickens Day or a day concentrating on the London fashion scene. We have walked through the tour with children and have been amazed at how many things they see that we, as adults, don't – like, for example, the ball shot which killed Lord Nelson.

Everything is detailed for you, so that you can either do the full day's tour or cut out what you don't want to do. We have included special events relating to the tours, places to eat, parks to rest in or for your children to let out energy, wheelchair access (but do telephone to say you are coming) and, of course, times of opening and closing, undergrounds, buses, prices, etc.

During the time we went to press, it became clear that a great majority of the museums, as well as Kew Gardens, were undergoing changes to their exhibition areas. For this reason, some places have not been included, such as Queen's House at Greenwich.

We strongly recommend that you get a Travelcard for use during your stay. A Two-Zone Travelcard for one week (which would cover seventy-five per cent of the tours) costs under £8 for an adult and under £2 for a child, considerably less than paying for your transport day by day.

To buy an adult Travelcard, take a passport photo to any underground station where you will get a Photocard and a Travelcard. The Photocard can then be used for subsequent Travelcards. To buy a child's Travelcard, take a passport or a birth certificate and photo to a Post Office to get a Photocard; then take the Photocard to any underground station to get the Travelcard.

Special Events

			Tours
Easter Monday Morning	London Harness Horse Parade	Regent's Park	14,30

	MAY		
9th	Oak-Apple Day	Royal Hospital, Chelsea	22
2nd Week	Royal Windsor Horse Show	Windsor Great Park	21
3rd Week	Chelsea Flower Show	Royal Hospital, Chelsea	22

	JUNE		
1st Week	Beating the Retreat	Horseguards Parade	4,8,12
1st or 2nd Week	Trooping the Colour	Horseguards Parade	4,8,12
3rd Week	Waterloo Banquet	Windsor Castle	21*
3rd Week	Procession of Knights of the Garter	Windsor Castle	21*

	JULY		
	Open Air Theatre	Regent's Park	14,30

	AUGUST		
Bank Holiday Weekend	Fair	Hampstead	15

OCTOBER

| 1st Week | Procession of Judges | Westminster Courts of Justice | 7,27 |

NOVEMBER

| Saturday closest to 9th | Lord Mayor's Show | City | 26 |
| Early in month | State Opening of Parliament | Buckingham Palace to Westminster | 4,7 |

* Windsor Castle Grounds will be closed except to those with entrance tickets. These can be obtained by writing to the Lord Chancellor, St James's Palace, London SW1.

Coding

£ – £1 and under	A – Adult
££ – up to £3	C – Child
£££ – £3 to £5	P – Pensioner
££££ – over £5	S – Student

TOUR 1
The Fire of London

1 All Hallows by the Tower, Byward St, London
EC3. Tel. (01) 481 2928
⊖ Tower Hill; Bus 23
09.00–18.00 Monday–Friday; 10.00–17.00 Saturday and
Sunday
Closed: Boxing Day and other days if necessary
Wheelchair/Shop/Food/Toilet

2 The Monument, Monument St, London EC3.
Tel. (01) 626 2717
⊖ Monument, Bank; Bus 10, 21, 23, 35, 40, 43, 44, 47,
48, 133, 501, 513
1 April–30 September: 09.00–18.00 Monday–Friday;
14.00–18.00 Saturday and Sunday
Summer lunchtime *closing*: Last entry 12.45, reopens
14.00
1 October–31 March: 09.00–16.00 Monday–Friday;
09.00–14.00 and 15.00–16.00 Saturday
A £, C £, OAP £, S (over 16) £

3 St Paul's Cathedral, St Paul's Churchyard, London
EC4. Tel. (01) 248 2705
⊖ St Paul's; Bus 4, 6, 8, 9, 11, 15, 23, 25, 141, 501, 513
Summer: 18.00; Winter 17.00
Guided Super Tours, 11.00 and 14.00 (weekdays), A ££,
C ££
Ambulatory, A £; *Crypt*, A £, C £; *Galleries*, A £, C £
Party rates for minimum of 20 adults and school parties
Wheelchair/Shop

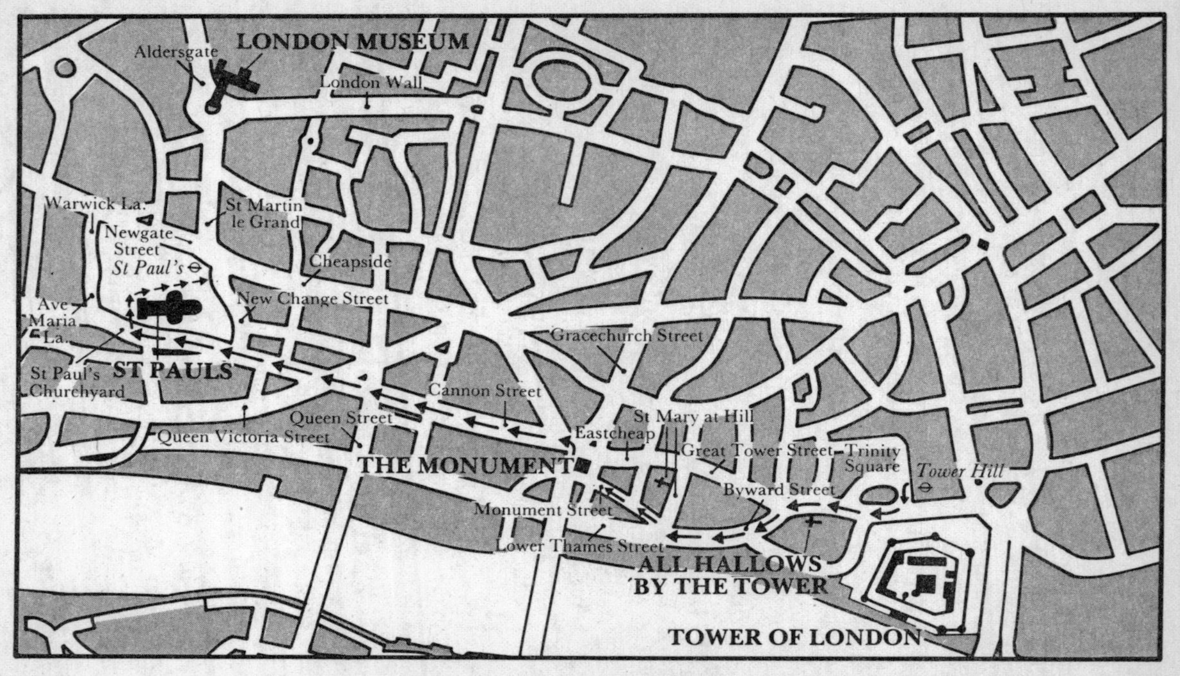

LONDON MUSEUM
Aldersgate
London Wall
Warwick La.
St Martin le Grand
Newgate Street
St Paul's
Cheapside
New Change Street
Ave Maria La.
Gracechurch Street
St Paul's Churchyard
ST PAULS
Cannon Street
St Mary at Hill
Eastcheap
Queen Street
Great Tower Street
Trinity Square
Queen Victoria Street
THE MONUMENT
Tower Hill
Byward Street
Monument Street
Lower Thames Street
ALL HALLOWS 'BY THE TOWER
TOWER OF LONDON

🚇 Tower Hill Underground

10.00 When you come out of Tower Hill underground you will immediately see a part of the old London Wall to your left. In front of you is the historic Tower of London, begun in the 11th Century by William the Conqueror (1028–87).

Behind you and to the right is Trinity Square where you will find Trinity House (Lighthouse Authority for England and Wales) and the Port of London Authority building.

Within Trinity Gardens is the site where, over three centuries, many people were executed for treason and crimes against the State. These include Sir Thomas More (1477–1535) and Guildford Dudley (d. 1554), the husband of Lady Jane Grey (1537–54). There is also a memorial to those men of the Merchant Navy and Fishing Fleets who died at sea for their country.

Cross Byward Street from Trinity Square and turn right. You can now see the beautiful spire of All Hallows by the Tower with its copper weathervane.

10.30 All Hallows by the Tower

The first church on this site was built in AD 700–800. The church standing here at the time of the Great Fire of 1666 was built in the 13th Century but it was not damaged then. The square brick tower, typical of the plainness of Puritan times, was built in the 1600s and was the only part of the church left standing after the bombings of World War II. It was here that Samuel Pepys (1633–1703) climbed the tower to survey the fire damage to the city – more than three-quarters of the city inside the old wall was destroyed.

Inside you will find a mariner's chapel with many model ships. Sometimes, before sailors went to sea, they made models of their ships and then left them in the church to bring good luck.

There are some very nice brasses which you can rub, and an underground chamber or vault called a crypt which can be visited with a guide. In the crypt you will see a Roman pavement found when the church was having its supports strengthened. There is also a model of Roman London and some Saxon stone crosses. In the baptistry (the place used for baptizing children) you will see a splendid font cover (a bowl holding the water used for baptizing) carved by Grinling Gibbons (1648–1721), which is made of one piece of lime.

11.00 When you come out of All Hallows, turn left and walk down Byward Street. Cross over the small road in front of you. Turn down some steps which take you down to Lower Thames Street. The ship which you see on the Thames is HMS *Belfast*. It is a cruiser, a heavily armed warship, built in 1939 and used in World War II.

Walk down Lower Thames Street, passing the Customs House on your left. The spire you see to your right belongs to St Dunstan in the East. Because the city was severely bombed during World War II, there is little old architecture left.

Cross Lower Thames Street and carry on, crossing St Mary at Hill Street, and then turn right into Monument Street. Pudding Lane, where the Great Fire began in the King's baker's premises, is to the left. Notice the ball of fire on top of the Monument.

11.30 The Monument

The Monument was constructed in 1671–7 to commemorate the Great Fire of 1666. It is exactly 202 feet high – the very same distance from the Monument to the bakery in Pudding Lane where the fire began.

Climb the 311 steps and you will be able to see where you have just come from. The most open view is down river to Tower Bridge. Unfortunately many tall buildings now spoil the view from the Monument.

12.00 There are a number of places to buy sandwiches between the Monument and St Paul's. Pubs and restaurants are there to serve the business community during the week and are mostly closed at weekends.

When you leave the Monument, continue to the top of Monument Street and then go down the steps to Cannon Street Underground; this will take you under the intersection. Turn left and go up the steps at the far end. You are now in Cannon Street, and if you look up the street, you will see St Paul's in the distance – your next stop. If you prefer to rest your legs, Bus 23 goes to St Paul's.

As you walk up Cannon Street, you will pass many banks. Cross Queen Street and carry on. Go down the steps to cross under Queen Victoria Street. When you get to the sign saying 'Leading to Bow Lane' turn right and then immediately left. Go up the steps to the right. Continue down Cannon Street.

When you get to St Paul's, carry on past it and then turn right. You will find the entrance up some stairs.

13.00 **St Paul's Cathedral**

For many years before old St Paul's was destroyed by the Great Fire of 1666, it suffered from misuse, smaller fires and damage in the Civil War. Christopher Wren (1632–1723) designed a cupola (a small dome) to help renovate the Cathedral, but the Great Fire intervened and he needed to design a completely new Cathedral. He submitted three plans, the first two of which were rejected. Finally, the foundation stone was laid in 1675 and it was finished in 1708.

Walk down the centre aisle. When you are almost at the dome, sit down and have a good look at the beautiful colours and ornamentation of the dome, nave and choir. There is nothing to equal it.

Visit the crypt, where you will see memorial tablets to many famous people such as Florence Nightingale (1820–1910), the poet and artist William Blake (1757–1827), the artist John Constable (1776–1837), and Sir Alexander Fleming (1881–1955), the man who discovered penicillin. You can see the tombs of Lord Nelson (1758–1805) and the Duke of Wellington (1769–1852). Just past the Duke of Wellington's tomb is the opening in the ceiling of the crypt through which the coffins are lowered after a funeral.

The Duke of Wellington's coffin was lowered into the crypt during his funeral and placed on top of Lord Nelson's tomb, the top having been taken off so that it was not damaged. Several years later when the Duke's tomb was finished, his coffin was placed inside it and the cover of Lord Nelson's tomb was replaced.

Don't forget to climb the stairs to the Whispering Gallery, where you can see frescoes of the life of St Paul. Frescoes are made by dissolving a pure pigment, such as an oxide, with water and then applying it to a wet lime-plastered wall. A chemical change then makes the colour permanent.

When leaving St Paul's, go to the right and walk round the other side of the Cathedral. Turn left and walk to St Paul's Underground.

Did You Spot?

1. What was on top of the weathervane of All Hallows by the Tower?
2. How many ships there were in All Hallows?
3. Whose statue was in front of the door to St Paul's?

Do You Know?

4. What the people who supported Oliver Cromwell were called?
5. Why Pepys (pronounced Peeps) was famous?
6. The name of Queen Victoria's husband?
7. What famous couple were recently married in St Paul's Cathedral?
8. Who Florence Nightingale was?
9. The nickname of the Duke of Wellington?

TOUR 2
The Ghost of Christmas Past

1 The Charles Dickens House, 48 Doughty St, London WC1. Tel. (01) 405 2127
⊖ Russell Square; Bus 5, 18, 19, 38, 45, 46, 55, 171, 172, 243, 259
10.00–17.00 Monday–Saturday; *Closed*: Sunday and Bank Holidays
A £, C £, P £, S £, Family ££; Shop

2 Lincoln's Inn, Chancery Lane, London WC1.
⊖ Chancery Lane; Bus 171

3 The Old Curiosity Shop, 13–14 Portsmouth St, London WC2. Tel. (01) 405 9891
⊖ Holborn; Bus 8, 9, 11, 13, 22, 25, 77
1 April–31 October: 09.00–17.30 Monday–Friday;
09.00–17.00 Saturday–Sunday and Holidays
1 November–31 March: 09.30–17.30 Monday–Friday;
09.30–17.00 Saturday–Sunday and Holidays;
Closed: Christmas Day

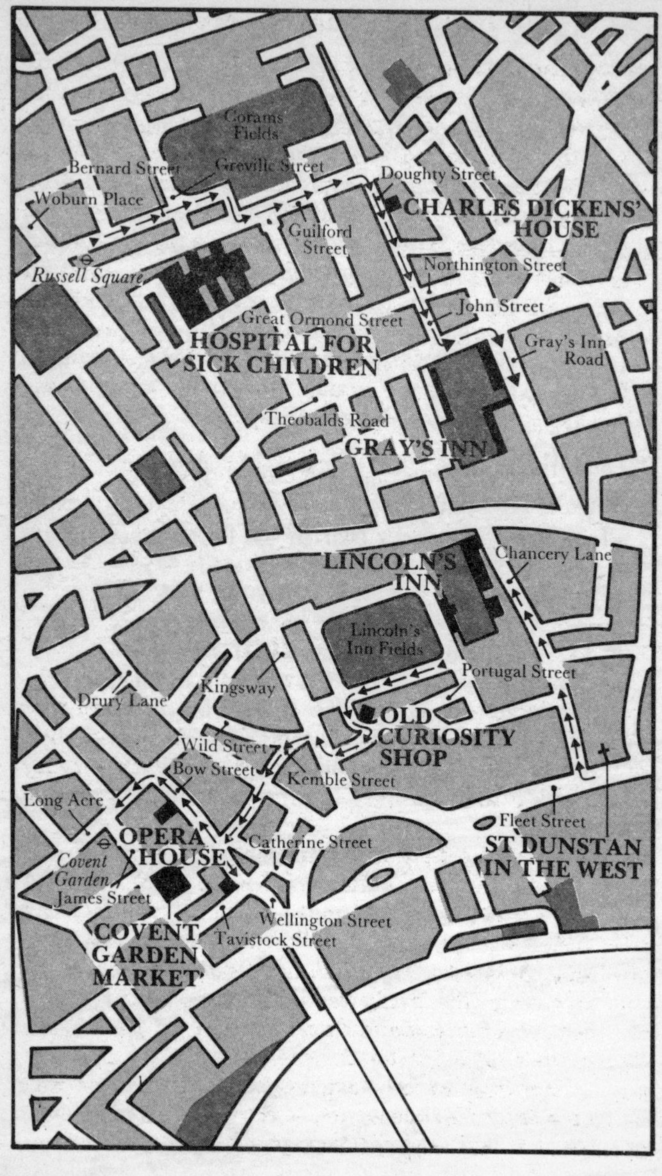

Corams Fields
Bernard Street
Greville Street
Doughty Street
Woburn Place
CHARLES DICKENS' HOUSE
Guilford Street
Northington Street
Russell Square
John Street
Great Ormond Street
Gray's Inn Road
HOSPITAL FOR SICK CHILDREN
Theobalds Road
GRAY'S INN
Chancery Lane
LINCOLN'S INN
Lincoln's Inn Fields
Portugal Street
Kingsway
Drury Lane
OLD CURIOSITY SHOP
Wild Street
Bow Street
Kemble Street
Long Acre
Fleet Street
OPERA HOUSE
Catherine Street
ST DUNSTAN IN THE WEST
Covent Garden
James Street
Wellington Street
COVENT GARDEN MARKET
Tavistock Street

⊖ Russell Square

10.30 When you leave Russell Square Underground, you will be in Bernard Street. Turn right. Cross Grenville Street and you will be approaching Coram Fields.

Thomas Coram (1668–1751), a sea captain who was connected with the State of Georgia in the United States, won a charter from George II (1683–1760) in 1739 to build accommodation and playing fields for children left to die in the streets. The hospital was demolished in 1926 and the children moved elsewhere. Although Thomas Coram's Hospital is gone, Great Ormond Street Children's Hospital is just south of Guilford Street.

Curve with the road and cross to the other side of Guilford Street. Go left and walk to Doughty Street. Cross it and then go right. Walk to No. 48. Push the bell on the left and wait for a buzzer to say the door is unlocked.

10.45 **The Charles Dickens House**

Charles Dickens (1812–70) was born in Portsmouth. His father at the time was a clerk in the Navy Pay Office and his mother's father, Charles Barrow, had just escaped to the Continent in order to avoid serving a prison sentence for the theft of £5000 from the Navy Board.

When Charles was 5 years old, his family moved to the dockyard at Chatham, where he went to school until their move to London when he was 11. His father was very much in debt when they left Chatham and everything they did not need was sent to a pawnshop. The family was so desperate that his father decided Charles should work when a job was offered in the blacking factory.

Shortly after he started working his father was arrested for bad debts and sent to prison at Marshalsea; his wife and the younger children joined him.

Charles had a room nearby. Salvation came when his father inherited enough money to pay his debts, allowing Charles to start school at the Wellington House Academy, where he stayed for two and a half years. When he was 14, he became an office boy for a firm of solicitors, learned shorthand and became a freelance reporter.

From this time on his life improved. An uncle started a newspaper called *Mirror of Parliament* and Charles went to work for him. Because of his speed and accuracy, he went on to become the star reporter for the *Morning Chronicle*. He fell in love with Maria Bedwell, courted her for four years, but finally ended the relationship because she was so unpredictable in her behaviour towards him.

He began writing, and produced his first sketch in the *Monthly Magazine*, others following. It was at this time that he began using the name Boz, which was the family name for brother. Dickens was asked to write some comic sketches for a new firm of publishers, Chapman & Hall, 20 monthly parts in all, and thus *Pickwick Papers* was begun.

He married Katherine Hogarth in 1836, and they lived in his rooms at Furnival Inn, which is no longer in existence. They moved to Doughty Street and Katherine's sister Mary came with them. When Mary died, Katherine's other sister Georgina moved in to help Katherine.

This Queen Anne house was the Dickens's home from 1837 to 1839. *Oliver Twist* and *Nicholas Nickleby* were written here. The Dickens' first child was only a few weeks old when they moved in, and while they lived in the house two more children were born. They subsequently moved to a house in Devonshire Place near Regent's Park, as this house was getting too small for their family.

When you get into the hallway, you will see drawings of many of Dickens's characters by F. Barnard.

Mr. Pickwick

You will go left into the **Dining Room** to pay. Here you will see the sideboard, which was bought in 1839, and a long-case clock which was owned by Moses Pickwick, whose name Dickens used for one of his most popular characters. There is a notice of Christmas Sports being held at Gads Hill by Charles Dickens and his son.

Now go into the **Morning Room** where you will see photographs and drawings of Georgina Hogarth. There is a cupboard of figures and plates commemorating Dickens's characters and a model of the Maypole Inn from the book *Barnaby Rudge*. There are also photographs of Charles Dickens's parents. He used his mother as a model for Mrs Nickleby and his father for Mr Micawber. You can see the tall desk which Dickens used when he was a clerk at Gray's Inn for a year. You will also see several paintings and drawings of his daughter Kate and various objects in a glass case, including a blacking pot similar to the one he put labels on in the factory.

As you go upstairs, you will see the Little Midshipman sign which Dickens used in *Dombey & Son*.

Go straight into the **Drawing Room**. The armchair, cane-bottomed chairs, small foot-stool, music stand and large table all belonged to Dickens.

Then enter the **Study**. It is thought that Dickens completed *Pickwick Papers* in this room, and that he also wrote *Oliver Twist* and *Nicholas Nickleby* here. The desk and chair were those he had at Gad's Hill. There is a drawing of Dickens on his death bed by John Everett Millais (1829–96).

Now go out into the hall and upstairs. Go into **Mary Hogarth's Room**, the room she died in of a heart attack at the age of 17. You can see a drawing of her by Phiz (H. K. Browne), one of the best illustrators of Dickens's books.

In **Dickens's Bedroom** are original drawings of H. K. Browne and other artists, and letters written by

Dickens. There are portraits of the parents of Maria Bedwell, Charles Dickens's first love.

The **Dressing Room** contains Dickens's reading desk, and marked copies of parts of his books which he used to prompt himself while giving readings. His public readings were very popular and he would often have whole audiences crying over the death of Little Nell. You can see several pictures of him giving readings.

Now go down to the **Basement**.

If you go straight on, you will see the **Library**, containing copies of all editions of Dickens's books, in all the languages they have been published in. The opposite end of the passage leads to a door to the left, where you can see the **Wine Cellar**. Back inside, and next to it, is the wash-room. There is a stone sink on a base of bricks and an oven-like fire, with a deep copper bowl and lid over it in which to boil and wash clothes. Water for baths had to be carried from this room to the room with the bath in it.

11.30 When you leave the house, walk to the left and continue to the end of the street. When the Dickens family moved in here, there were gates at either end, and guards to keep unwanted people out.

You will see Gray's Inn, where Dickens worked for a year when he was about 14. Cross the intersection and walk to a bus stop on Gray's Inn Road across from Gray's Inn. (This stop is a request stop and you will have to wave the bus down.)

Take a 171 bus to Chancery Lane. It is a difficult journey to keep track of because of the one-way systems. Although you want Chancery Lane, you will get off the bus on Fleet Street, across from St Dunstan in the West. If you look at the church you can see a statue of Queen Elizabeth I (1533–1605) with an orb and sceptre.

Cross Fleet Street at the lights. If you look back across the street you may see a man in a long-tailed grey suit – the doorman of Messrs Hoare the Bankers.

The present **St Dunstan in the West** was built in the 1800s. John Donne (1572–1631) was Vicar here. He was a poet, a priest, and Dean of St Paul's. Ancestors of George Washington (1732–99), first President of the United States, are buried here also.

As you walk along, you will see some beautiful old buildings on the left. One is Prince Henry's Room, and the Tudor building is Staple Inn, once used for first-year law students. Before that it was the home of a wool merchant.

There are pubs and restaurants on Fleet Street where you can get something to eat.

Cross Chancery Lane and turn right. Walk straight ahead until you see the Sun Alliance offices to your right. To your left is the main entrance to Lincoln's Inn. If you look above the door you can see the centre arms of Henry VIII (1491–1547).

12.30 **Lincoln's Inn**

Lincoln's Inn is one of the Inns of Court and dates back, at least, to 1422. The name comes from the Earl of Lincoln, who had a town house (inn) here in the 1300s.

Walk through the **Old Buildings**, which are Tudor, refaced with brick, and go to the left through the Arch. Veer to the right. The next square you come to is New Square, built in the 1600s. Dickens worked as a clerk here when he was about 11, as an apprentice to a Mr Molley. He also set the opening scene of *Bleak House* in the Old Hall of Lincoln's Inn, where the case of Jarndyce vs. Jarndyce was being heard.

Walk straight past the court and go out of the gate into Lincoln's Inn Fields. To the left, you will see the Law Courts. Continue straight past Lincoln's Inn

Fields on your right. Also, on the left, you will see the Public Records Office, the Nuffield College of Surgical Sciences, the Royal College of Surgeons, and the Imperial Cancer Research Fund. Turn left on Portsmouth Street and a few paces on you will find the Old Curiosity Shop.

13.00 The Old Curiosity Shop

This house was built in the late 1500s. Walk in and have a look at the interesting jumble of things here – first editions of Dickens's novels, silver, plates, etc. It is said that Dickens used this shop as the model for the one in his book.

13.30 When you have finished in the shop, walk to the end of Portsmouth Street and turn right into Portugal Street. You will arrive at Kingsway. Kingsway is always very busy with traffic; there is a tunnel which feeds traffic into the road from your left after the road divider. Find a safe place to cross and be particularly careful when crossing the second part of the road.

Walk down Kemble Street and, when the street divides, go to the left. Continue walking and cross Drury Lane. You are now walking alongside Covent Garden Opera House. Cross Katherine Street and turn left at Wellington Street. You can see Covent Garden Market in front of you.

Cross Tavistock Street. On the corner is No. 26 Wellington Street where, in 1850, Dickens started his weekly newspaper called *Household Words*. This title was later changed to *All The Year Round*, which was still being published from this address in the 1880s.

Retrace your steps up Wellington Street, which becomes Bow Street. Walk to Long Acre and then turn left. Covent Garden Underground is on the corner of James Street and Long Acre.

Did You Spot?

1. The man sitting on the tall stool in a drawing? Who is he?
2. The arm hanging on the wall? What does the person do?
3. What was on the table in the Drawing Room? What is it?

Do You Know?

4. What sports are being organized as Christmas games?
5. What book uses the name of Moses Pickwick?
6. How they emptied water in the basement after washing clothes?
7. What is unusual about one figure of Dickens?
8. Which years are considered to be Tudor? 1400–1500, 1500–1600, or 1600–1700?
9. Who Wellington Street is named after?

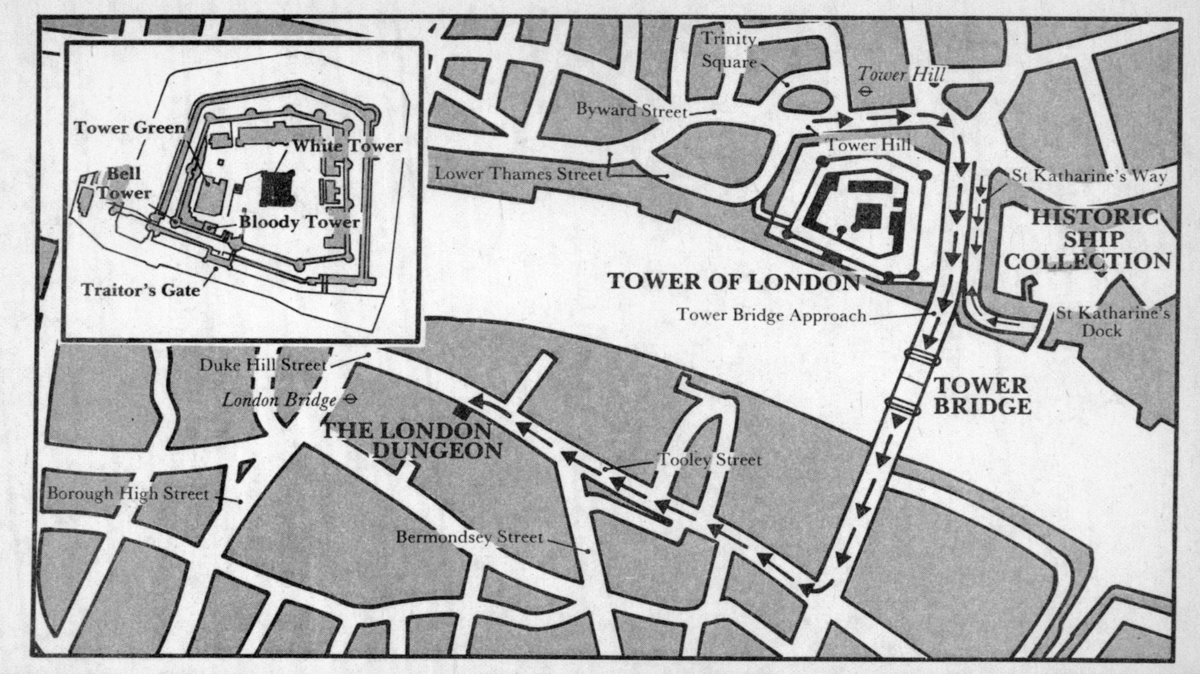

Trinity Square
Tower Hill
Byward Street
Tower Hill
Lower Thames Street
St Katharine's Way
HISTORIC SHIP COLLECTION
St Katharine's Dock
Tower Green
White Tower
Bell Tower
Bloody Tower
Traitor's Gate
TOWER OF LONDON
Tower Bridge Approach
TOWER BRIDGE
Duke Hill Street
London Bridge
THE LONDON DUNGEON
Tooley Street
Borough High Street
Bermondsey Street

TOUR 3
Dungeons and Hangings at the Tower

1 H.M. Tower of London, London EC3
● Tower Hill; Bus 23
Boat from Westminster Pier, leaves every 20 minutes.
Only from Easter to September
Summer: 09.30–17.00; Winter 09.30–16.00 (last tickets
sold)
Tower: March–October: A ££, C 5–15 ££, P ££;
    November–February: A ££, C 5–15 £, P £;
    Closed: Sundays from November to February
Jewel Tower: March–October: A £, C 5–15 £, P £;
     November–February: A £, C 5–15 £, P £
Limited Wheelchair/Shop/Food/Toilet

2 St Katharine's Docks, London by the Tower,
London E1
Historic Ship Collection. Tel. (01) 481 0043
● Tower Hill

3 Tower Bridge
● Tower Hill
April–October: 10.00–18.30;
November–March: 10.00–16.45.
A ££, C £

4 The London Dungeon, 28–34 Tooley Street, SE1.
Tel. (01) 403 0606
● London Bridge; Bus 47, 70
April–September 10.00–17.45;
October–March 10.00–16.30 (last admission)
A £££, C ££, P ££
Wheelchair/Food/Toilet/Shop

Fourteenth-century armour, from the
Tower of London

⊖ Tower Hill
Boat From Westminster Pier every 20 min. 10.20 to
1600/1800 hrs.

09.15 It is best to arrive for a visit to the Tower as early as
possible. The summer holidays, and weekends
especially, are very busy and there are often long
queues. Tours lasting about an hour are available
every 30 minutes and are included in your price of
admission. They are given by Yeoman Warders and
are interesting to young and old alike.

Walk to Byward Street from Tower Hill Underground; turn left and go down the steps which go
under the road (there is also a ramp). If you are lucky
you may see a one-man band in the subway. On
leaving the subway, go to the right and follow the
moat around the Tower. When the moat was built, it
was much deeper than it is now.

09.30 ## H.M. Tower of London
The building of the Tower of London (the White
Tower) was begun in 1077 at the behest of William
the Conqueror (1028–87), as he wanted a strong
defence on the River Thames. It was finished 20 years
later.

The **Bell Tower** was built about 1100–1200 and is
famous as the prison of Princess Elizabeth, later
Queen Elizabeth I (1533–1603). Also imprisoned here
was Sir Thomas More (1477–1535), who died on Tower
Hill.

Traitor's Gate is where, in the 16th Century,
prisoners entered the Tower after their trials at
Westminster. Many famous people passed through
these gates – Anne Boleyn (1507–36), Catherine
Howard (1520–42), Edward Seymour, Duke of Somerset (d. 1551), and Princess Elizabeth – among others.

The **Bloody Tower** is called this because it may

have been the place Henry Percy, 8th Earl of Northumberland (d. 1585), committed suicide. It is also rumoured that the little princes, Edward (V) and Richard, sons of Edward IV, were murdered here in 1483. Sir Walter Raleigh (1554–1613) was imprisoned in this Tower for 12 years, and you can see rooms furnished in the fashion of the time when he was a prisoner.

Tower Green is where the royal private executions took place. Executed here were William, Lord Hastings (d. 1483), Anne Boleyn (d. 1536), Margaret, Countess of Salisbury (d. 1541), Catherine Howard (d. 1542), Jane, Viscountess Rochford (d. 1542), Lady Jane Grey (d. 1554), and Robert Devereux, Earl of Essex (d. 1601). Several of them are buried in the Chapel Royal of St Peter ad Vincula, but you cannot see inside this chapel unless you take a tour.

There are many carved inscriptions in **Beauchamp Tower**, which was a prison from the 14th Century. Some have been moved there from other areas of the Tower.

In 1241 the **White Tower** was a royal apartment for Henry III (1207–72). There were many famous prisoners lodged here also, including David, King of Scots (1084–1153), John the Good, King of France (1319–64), Charles of Blois and the Duc d'Orléans (1387–1422), who was captured by Henry V during the Battle of Agincourt (1415). Be sure to see the Chapel of St John, built about 1080, which is a perfect example of a Norman chapel.

The White Tower is now a museum of armoury. The museum was begun by Henry VIII (1491–1547) and each floor contains examples of armour, including Henry VIII's. The galleries are organized as follows: Sporting, Tournament, Medieval, 16th Century, Tudor and 17th Century.

There are about 40 **Yeoman Warders** at the Tower. You will see them on normal duty in blue uniforms designed by Queen Victoria (1819–1901) in 1858. The State red and gold uniforms, only worn for important occasions, date from 1552.

The **Crown Jewels** were once kept at Westminster, but after a theft in 1303 most of them were sent to the Tower for safe keeping. Oliver Cromwell (1599–1658) ordered that the Crown Jewels be melted down or sold. The jewels you see now are mostly reproductions using as many of the original jewels as possible.

You can see, among others, St Edward's Crown, thought to be the crown of Edward the Confessor (1003–66) and the Imperial State Crown for the coronation of Queen Victoria, which contains a ruby which may have been given to the Black Prince (1330–76) in 1367.

When you come out of the Tower, go back to Tower Hill and walk past the north side of the Tower. Carry on right, going south towards Tower Bridge. St Katharine's Docks are signposted.

You are crossing under Tower Bridge Road. Walk through the gardens of the World Trade Building. Then turn left into the road which goes along the side of the Tower Hotel.

13.00 St Katharine's Docks

Now you can explore St Katharine's Docks, where you will find an exhibition of historic ships and also a few shops. If you didn't bring sandwiches with you, there are places where you can buy something to eat, such as the Dickens Inn.

After your visit, leave St Katharine's by the river side of Tower Hotel. When you reach Tower Bridge go up the stairs directly across from the traffic lights. This takes you up to the bridge.

14.00 Tower Bridge

Tower Bridge was built in 1894. If you like, you can do a tour of the different levels of the bridge.

If not, walk across Tower Bridge and continue walking until you reach Tooley Street. Turn right and walk east. It is a short walk to the London Dungeon, which you will see on your left.

14.30 The London Dungeon

The London Dungeon has set exhibits of the hair-raising living conditions of Medieval England. Although the museum is very ghoulish, it is interesting if you put it in the context of what you have learned about the Tower during your visit there.

When you leave the London Dungeon, continue walking in the same direction on Tooley Street. Cross Joiner Street and then go left to London Bridge Underground.

Did You Spot?

1. Something on Tower Green to remind you of the executions held there?
2. The statue by the Thames at St Katharine's Dock? What was it?
3. What was holding up a window of the Shipwright's Arms in Tooley St?

Do You Know?

4. What bird is mentioned in a legend about the Tower?
5. What the gate is called through which prisoners entered the Tower?
6. Why there was a tower called Lion Tower?
7. Who wrote a book while a prisoner at the Tower?
8. When the guns on Tower Wharf are fired?
9. What is the name of the torture instrument invented by Sir Leonard Skevington, who was Lieutenant of the Tower in the reign of Henry VIII?
10. How the plague got to England?

TOUR 4
Changing of the Guard and the Royal Mews

1 Changing of the Guard, St James's Palace,
London SW1.
⊖ Green Park; Bus 9, 14, 19, 22, 25, 38, 55
11.00 daily

**2 Changing of the Guard, Buckingham
Palace,** London SW1.
⊖ Green Park, St James's Park; Bus 9, 14, 19, 22, 25, 38,
55
1 April–12 August: 11.30 daily
14 August–31 March: 11.30 every other day
These dates can change and should be checked with a
tourist office.

3 The Queens Gallery, Buckingham Palace, London
SW1.
⊖ Green Park, St James's Park; Bus 9, 14, 19, 22, 25, 38,
55
11.00–17.00 Tuesday–Saturday; 14.00–17.00 Sunday.
Closed: Mondays, Good Friday, 24, 25 December, between
exhibitions
A £, C £, P £; Shop

4 The Royal Mews, Buckingham Palace, London SW1.
Tel. (01) 930 4832 ext. 634
⊖ Green Park, St James's Park; Bus 2, 11, 16, 25, 29, 36,
52, 134
14.00–16.00 Wednesday–Thursday; *Closed*: Monday–
Tuesday, Friday–Sunday and the week of Ascot
A £, C £, P £, Handicapped – no charge

Special Events
Beating the Retreat, Horseguards Parade
1st week of June, Tuesday, 18.30, Wednesday and
Thursday, 21.30

**Trooping the Colour for the Queen's Official
Birthday**, Horseguards Parade
1st or 2nd Saturday of June, depending on the Queen's
calendar. At 10.00 guards begin to assemble at
Buckingham Palace. The Queen leaves the Palace for
Horseguards at 10.45 and returns to the Palace at 12.15;
she goes onto the balcony at about 13.00.

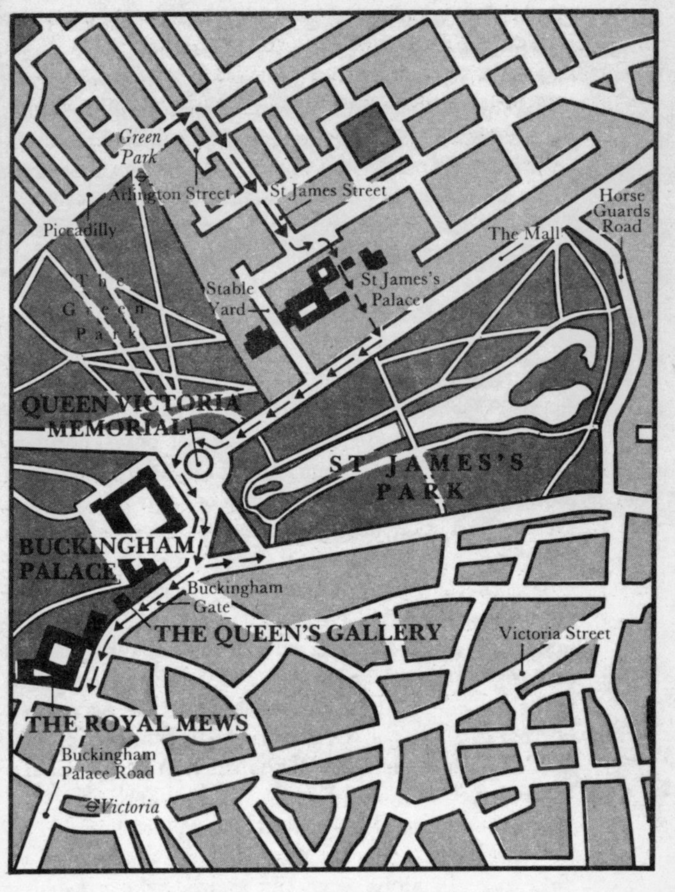

Green Park
Arlington Street
St James Street
Horse Guards Road
Piccadilly
The Mall
The Green Park
Stable Yard
St James's Palace
QUEEN VICTORIA MEMORIAL
ST JAMES'S PARK
BUCKINGHAM PALACE
Buckingham Gate
THE QUEEN'S GALLERY
Victoria Street
THE ROYAL MEWS
Buckingham Palace Road
Victoria

⊖ Green Park

10.30 Leave the underground through the exit marked South Side Piccadilly. Once on the street turn right and walk past the Ritz Hotel, cross Arlington Street and continue straight ahead. Turn right down St James's Street. Notice the opulent style of the houses on Piccadilly and St James's. In the last century, there were a large number of clubs on these streets.

As you get to the end of St James's, notice Berry Bros and Rudd Ltd at No. 3; they have been wine merchants since the 17th Century.

St James's Palace is directly in front of you.

11.00 St James's Palace

In 1529, when Henry VIII (1491–1547) got rid of Cardinal Wolsey (1475–1530), he not only appropriated Hampton Court, but also York Place which was along the river at Whitehall and belonged to Wolsey. Henry VIII also acquired what is now St James's Park and built St James's Palace as a hunting lodge.

The small leaded windows on the right belong to the Chapel Royal. Charles 1 (1600–1649) spent his last night at St James's, and in the morning walked across St James's Park to the Banqueting House to be beheaded. All foreign ambassadors are accredited (authorized) to the Court of St James and proclamations are made from the balcony on Friary Court. Members of the Royal Family still live here.

The Changing of the Guard takes place here before the changing at Buckingham Palace. You should be able to walk along with the guards who are being relieved of duty as they go to Buckingham Palace to join the guards leaving there. You will certainly have a better view of the changing here as Buckingham Palace can have people five and six deep trying to peer through the fence.

There are several foot regiments which rotate guarding the Queen:

The **Coldstream Guards**, from Coldstream in Scotland, are the oldest regiment and had their beginnings with General George Monck (1608–70).

Charles II (1630–85) formed the **Scots Guards** in 1642 which, although split up during the Civil War, were reformed as part of the Scottish Army in 1660.

The **Grenadier Guards** began as King Charles II's personal guard when he was forced into exile after his father's (Charles I) execution in 1649.

The **Irish Guards** were formed by Queen Victoria (1819–1901) in 1900 to honour them for their valour in the Boer Wars.

King George V (1865–1936) formed the **Welsh Guards** in 1915 so that all areas of the United Kingdom were represented.

The easiest way to tell which regiment is changing guard is to look at the buttons on their tunics. They also have different plumes in their bear-skin head-dresses.

Head-dress Plume

Red	None	White	Blue	Green & White
Buttons				
Coldstream Guards	Scots Guards	Grenadier Guards	Irish Guards	Welsh Guards

Walk down the side of St James's Palace, passing Friary Court on your right. Across the street is

Queen's Chapel, built for Queen Henrietta Maria (1609–69), wife of Charles I. The Chapel is only open for Sunday morning survice and has choirboys who wear costumes of scarlet and gold.

Continue walking until you arrive at the Mall, and then go right. You are walking towards Buckingham Palace. At the next road to the right, walk down to the gates and look through – you will see Clarence House, the home of Elizabeth, the Queen Mother.

Go back to the Mall and continue walking towards Buckingham Palace. You may see the Queen's Life Guards coming up the Mall from Whitehall to return to their barracks at Hyde Park.

You will begin to see the 82-foot-high Queen Victoria Memorial. When it was built in 1910, the memorial was found to be too tall for Buckingham Palace, so the Palace wall facing it was heightened with stone.

Follow the pavement past the gates to Green Park and go as far as the traffic lights. If you look at the keyholes in the gates, you will see the insignia of King Edward VII (1841–1910). Cross the street at the traffic lights.

11.30 **Buckingham Palace**

The original part of Buckingham Palace was built in the 18th Century by the Duke of Buckingham. It was bought by George III (1738–1820) in 1762 to present to his new wife, Charlotte. It remained much as it had been when it was built until George IV (1762–1830) decided to renovate it. It was not completed until 1837, the year Queen Victoria became Queen, and she moved in shortly afterwards.

While you are watching the Changing of the Guard, be sure to notice the balcony where the Royal Family stand to wave to the crowds of well-wishers on special occasions.

12.15 Now walk past the Palace. Cross Buckingham Palace
Road at the lights. Be careful! – there are no lights
for pedestrians. Cross left into Birdcage Walk, so
named because Charles II had birdcages along the
walk. On your right is the Guards Museum, Shop and
Wellington Barracks. Notice the new Chapel. In June
1944, 120 Guardsmen were killed in a direct hit on
the chapel. Continue walking until you come to traffic
lights. Cross and go into St James's Park.

12.45 ## St James's Park

As mentioned before, Henry VIII acquired St James's
Park. At the time of the dissolution of the monasteries
he acquired further land, and eventually had a hunting area stretching from St James's Park to
Hampstead Heath in the north. James I (1566–1625)
installed a collection of animals, including an eleph-
ant which was given a gallon of wine every morning
during cold weather. Charles II opened the park to
the public and could often be found strolling about
and even taking a swim in the canal. In 1830, John
Nash (1752–1835) redesigned the Park.

As you enter you will see a children's playground
on your right. The park is full of birds (over 20
species) and there are benches and seats everywhere.
During the summer there are concerts at the bandstand, and every afternoon, if you go to the bird-
keeper's cottage at Duck Pond, you can watch him
feeding fish to the birds. Horseguards Parade is at
the opposite end to where you entered the Park.

Go back to Birdcage Walk and cross to the other
side. Return the way you came until you reach the
intersection. Cross and go down Buckingham Palace
Road past the side of the Palace. You will come to the
Queen's Gallery.

The Queen's Gallery

This gallery contains changing exhibitions of collections of the Queen. Recent ones have included Royal Paintings and one on Fabergé.

Continue down the road. The Mews are just a bit further.

14.00 The Royal Mews

As you enter the square of the Mews, you will see the State Coach directly in front (during the winter it is not exhibited). It is a fairy-like coach all in gold with hats, plumes, horns, shells and lion's heads.

Carry on round the courtyard. Go through the central arch and to the right. Here are some of the coaches. Notice the lights on the posts – they are gas lamps. There are landaus, the Glass Coach, Alexandra's State Coach, Queen Victoria's last coach, sociables, Edward VII's town coach, the Irish State Coach, an Ascot landau, Oppenheimers and barouches.

Go out and cross to the other side to the stables. You can see some of the horses used to pull the coaches. Not all of them are here as the horses are grazed at Hampton Court or Windsor. These horses are taken out every day for exercise and are only in these stables while the Mews are open.

The next stop is the room containing tackle, and after that a room containing various saddles, whips, photos of the horses being used, rosettes and cups won by members of the Royal Family.

When you leave the Mews, go right and down Buckingham Palace Road, crossing to the other side at Victoria Street. Then cross Victoria Street and go left to Victoria Underground.

Did You Spot?

1. Where the guard takes shelter when it rains?
2. Whether the Queen Mother had a guard on duty?
3. What animal was sitting on top of the centre gate?
4. What was at the very top of Queen Victoria's statue?
5. What the decoration was on top of the State Coach?

Do You Know?

6. Which guard has buttons evenly spaced?
7. Which guards you saw changing?
8. What was different about Queen Victoria's coach?

TOUR 5
Dinosaurs, Bustles and the Giraffe Piano

1 The Natural History Museum, Cromwell Rd,
South Kensington, London SW7. Tel. (01) 589 6323
⊖ South Kensington; Bus 14, 30, 49, 74
10.00–18.00 Monday–Saturday; 14.30–18.00 Sunday
Closed: 1st Monday May, 24, 25, 26 December, 1 January
Wheelchair/Shop/Food/Toilet

2 The Victoria and Albert Museum, Cromwell
Rd, South Kensington, London SW7. Tel. (01) 589 6371
⊖ South Kensington; Bus 14, 30, 49, 74
10.00–17.50 Monday–Thursday, Saturday; 14.30–17.50
Sunday
Closed: Friday, 1st Monday May, 24, 25, 26 December,
1 January
Wheelchair/Shop/Food/Toilet
A ££

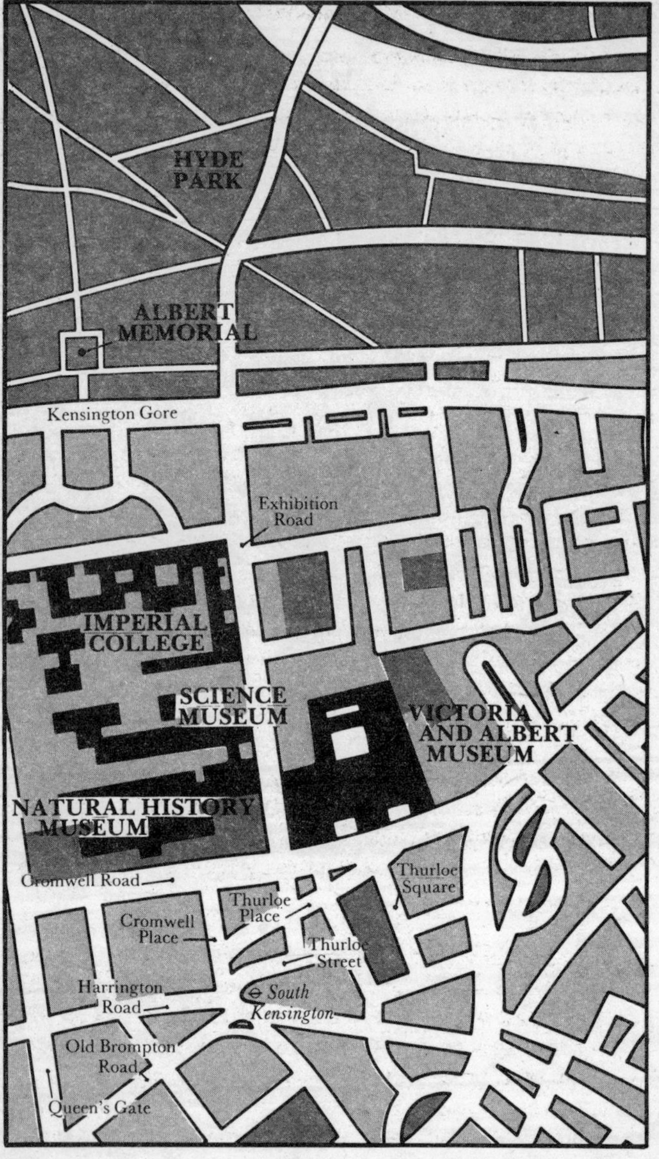

HYDE PARK
ALBERT MEMORIAL
Kensington Gore
Exhibition Road
IMPERIAL COLLEGE
SCIENCE MUSEUM
VICTORIA AND ALBERT MUSEUM
NATURAL HISTORY MUSEUM
Cromwell Road
Thurloe Square
Cromwell Place
Thurloe Place
Thurloe Street
Harrington Road
South Kensington
Old Brompton Road
Queen's Gate

⊖ South Kensington

Follow the signs for the Museums and use the subway, which is signposted.

    Note: The subway is open on weekdays from 07.00 to 21.00

        Sunday from 14.00 to 20.00

When you leave the subway you will go straight into the grounds of the Natural History Museum. It is a pink and blue-grey building, with animal sculptures above the windows.

10.00 **The Natural History Museum**

When you walk into the **Central Hall** you are immediately confronted with two large dinosaurs. Imagine what it would be like to see that long tail swishing about; and it has such a small head on a very long neck.

In Bay 1 there is a commentary on the ground-floor exhibits, and in the areas around the main entrance the exhibits are divided into two distinct sides: on one side are living species and on the other are the extinct. You will be able to push buttons to sort animals into groups according to features.

Go back to the entrance and turn left. This will take you into an exhibition of **fossils**. You can see the ancestors of horses, oxen, dogs and cats.

To the right of the entrance are the exhibits of **birds**, including the dodo. This bird came from Mauritius and is now extinct. It was very fat and had such small wings that it couldn't fly, and was easily hunted.

Turn right and go into the **insect** Section, which is brilliant with colour. You can learn about silk moths, honey bees and ants. Then go into the **marine invertebrates**, proceeding left.

When you get to the end go into the **whale** exhibition. As you walk into this room, you will hear recordings of echo-soundings by whales. There is a mammoth blue whale hanging from the ceiling. Go up the stairs to the left. These lead you to an exhibition of whales – their feeding habits, echo-locating, and camouflage colours.

Go down by the same steps and out of the whale hall, straight into the **human biology** Section.

Here you can stand in front of mirrors which make you tall, fat, thin and short. You can also pull a lever and see what nerves are instructing the muscles to exert themselves. It is possible to telephone for a recorded message from a scientist explaining how his work relates to the exhibition. Finally, you can test yourself on what is called your short-term memory, which means how much you can remember shortly after learning it.

On the **first floor** are exhibitions of African mammals, the origin of the species, minerals, rocks and gemstones, meteorites, and human's place in evolution.

12.30 If you haven't brought a packed lunch, there is a café and a snack bar in the Natural History Museum, or there is a very good cafeteria in the Victoria and Albert Museum – your next stop.

Go back the way you came but when you get to the tunnel, go up the stairs to the street. Cross Exhibition Road. The entrance to the Victoria and Albert Museum is to your left a bit further on.

1.30 The Victoria and Albert Museum

Walk into the Museum, pass the shop and turn left. You will be passing through exhibitions of Islam (47c); Indian Sculpture (47b); and South East Asia (47a). Turn right into the **Dress Collection**.

The Dress Collection is splendid, with examples of clothes from 1500 to the 1980s. There are men's suits

Day dress, 1858, from the Victoria
and Albert Museum

and dressing gowns, evening dresses, coats, evening clothes, soft day dresses, the ruffles and lace of the 1700s and the sleek 1920s. You are told what material the clothes are made of, whether the lace is machine or bobbin and, in many cases, who wore the clothes. There are some dolls with doll clothes as well as fans, shoes and hats. You may see students doing drawings of the clothes for their art courses.

Now go up the stairs in the Dress Collection. These will take you to the **Musical Instruments Gallery**.

To see the wind instruments in the green cases, you need to push a button, which turns on a light. There is a Giraffe Piano, which has a drum and bells inside the cabinet (needed for a type of music which was popular at one time).

There is a Serpent wind instrument, which was used for the music in churches from 16th to 19th Centuries. There are disc, revolver and orchestra musical boxes.

Various forms of harpsicord are here. All three types of harpsicord had their strings plucked by quills rather than hit by a hammer as with pianos.

The earliest type of harpsicord is a virginal, which was just a box which normally sat on a table. It had one note to each string and the strings ran parallel to the keys.

The next form is a spinet, which also had one note per string, but was not in the shape of a box. It was wing-shaped and the strings ran at a 45-degree angle.

Then came the proper harpsicord which had two or more notes per string; it was wing-shaped like the spinet, but the strings ran out directly from the keys.

You can also see an oboe which belonged to the composer Rossini (1792–1868), a dancing master's fiddle which belonged to the eldest son of the French King Louis XIV (Sun King) (1638–1716) and a violin made by the most famous violin maker of all.

When you have finished in the Musical Instrument

Gallery, go back down the steps and out of the Dress Collection through the exit which is near case 59. Then go left.

You will go through Gallery 21, High Renaissance. Near the steps you will see on the left a chess board made in the 1500s, and above you a beautiful lantern from Venice in 1570.

Go up the stairs and through the doors to the right. You are now in the **Rodin Sculpture Gallery**.

Auguste Rodin (1840–1917) was a French sculptor greatly influenced by the great Italian painter Michelangelo (1475–1564). Because of the realism of his work he had a certain amount of trouble when he delivered his finished sculptures. Two examples which caused an uproar were a nude statue of Victor Hugo (1802–85) and one of Honoré de Balzac (1799–1850) in his dressing gown.

Now go down the stairs, turn right and down the ramp and into the Boilerhouse Exhibition area. The exhibitions here change about every two months and can be very interesting. Recently there have been exhibitions on shopping bags, cars and ergonomics (the design of things you use, like machines and tools, with regard to people's physical and psychological needs).

There is an exit in the middle of the Rodin Sculpture Gallery. But if you are not too tired, there are still many interesting things to look at, like the Great Bed of Ware in Gallery 63, which was made in the 1500s and is 8¾ feet tall and 10½ feet wide.

When you leave the Museum, cross Exhibition Road and return by way of the pedestrian subway.

Did You Spot?

1. What forms the largest group of insects?
2. What leaf the silkworm eats?
3. What was unusual on an orchestra box which was on a lower shelf?

Do You Know?

4. What word describes a dead organism which has turned to stone?
5. What our closest fossil relative is?
6. Why sperm whales have been hunted so much over the years?
7. What sends messages to your arm to tell it to move?
8. What women used to make their dresses stick out at the back?
9. Who is the most famous violin maker?

TOUR 6
Toys, Time and Fashion

1 The Bethnal Green Museum of Childhood,
Cambridge Heath Rd, London E2. Tel. (01) 980 2415/
3204/4315
⊖ Bethnal Green; Bus 6, 6A, 8, 8A, 35, 55, 106, 253
10.00–18.00 Monday–Thursday, Saturday; 14.30–18.00
Sunday
Closed: Friday, 1st Monday in May, 24, 25, 26 December,
1 January.
Wheelchair/Shop/Toilet

2 The Geffrye Museum, Kingsland Rd, London E2.
Tel. (01) 739 8368/9893
⊖ Old Street; Bus 11, 11A, 48, 67, 149, 243
10.00–17.00 Tuesday–Saturday; 14.00–17.00 Sunday
Closed: Monday (except Bank Holidays when open
10.00–1700)
Wheelchair/Shop/Toilet

3 Bunhill Burial Fields, City Rd, London EC1
⊖ Old Street; Bus 5, 55, 83, 84, 243
October–March: 07.30–16.00 week, 09.30–16.00 weekend
April–September: 07.30–15.00 week, 09.30–sunset
weekend

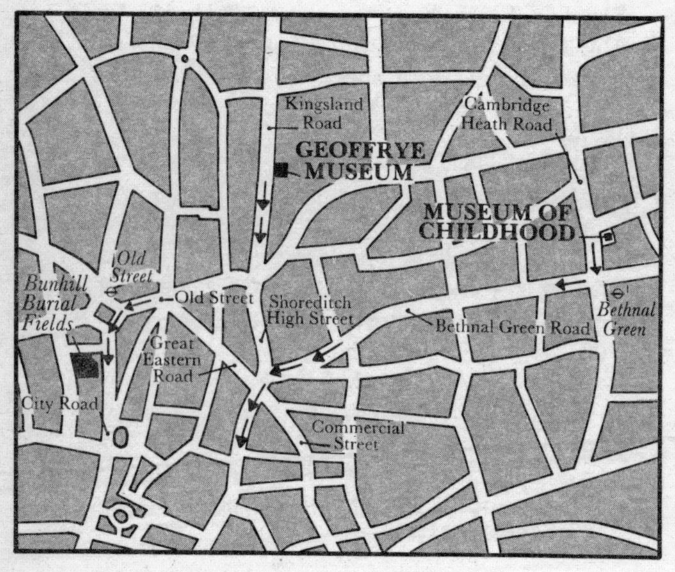

Kingsland
Road
Cambridge
Heath Road
GEOFFRYE
MUSEUM
MUSEUM OF
CHILDHOOD
Old
Street
Bunhill
Burial
Fields
Old Street
Shoreditch
High Street
Bethnal Green Road
Bethnal
Green
Great
Eastern
Road
City Road
Commercial
Street

⊖ Bethnal Green Underground

Because this trip involves a lot of walking to get the buses required for the tour, it is unsuitable for very young children.

The museum is signposted at Bethnal Green Underground and will be on your right.

The Bethnal Green Museum of Childhood is part of the Victoria and Albert Museum. The original building, of iron and glass, was constructed to hold temporarily items shown at the Great Exhibition of 1851. It was moved to this site in 1872 and an outer brick shell was added.

10.00 The Bethnal Green Museum of Childhood

It would be best to start at the top of the museum and work your way down. On the top floor, you will find the decorative arts with examples of porcelain, glass, and ornamentally carved furniture.

The remainder of the space is taken up with an exhibition of clothes, shoes, socks, hats and umbrellas. One of the exhibits dates from 1842 and is the school wardrobe belonging to a little girl named Henrietta Byron. Another is a girl's silk outfit made in 1741 from silk spun in Spitalfields by Huguenot refugees from France. There is also a collection of wedding dresses covering the last three centuries.

On the next two floors down are the exhibits of doll's houses, their furniture and toys. There are several examples of butcher's shops and a beautiful house built in 1673 in Nuremburg. Notice the baby in its walker and the big bed with the step up to it.

Be sure to look at the huge model of a circus with spectators, cafés, and an animal exhibition area. There are model trains, stage coaches with the luggage piled on top, mechanical toys and rocking horses.

The Museum is filled with toys children have loved to play with over the years.

The doll collection is very good, beginning with the earliest crude wooden dolls and moving on to those made of porcelain. You will see dolls made by famous makers such as Jumeau, Armand Marseille and Simon & Halbig who, in conjunction with Kammer and Reinhardt, made the character dolls of the late 1800s and early 1900s. For many years, a family named Powell dressed dolls in copies of their favourite clothes, or in new fashions for riding bicycles or playing tennis.

12.00 There is a park next to the Museum where you can eat a packed lunch, or you can eat at a pub across the street from the Geffrye Museum which serves food and has outside seating. Remember that pubs are open from 11.00 to 15.00 during the day.

13.00 When you leave the museum, go left and towards Bethnal Green Underground. Cross Cambridge Heath Road at the traffic lights and then walk up Bethnal Green High Street towards Shoreditch until you reach the first bus stop. Take a No. 8 bus to Shoreditch High Street.

Get off the bus, walk to the corner and turn left into Shoreditch High Street. Walk to the traffic lights and cross Shoreditch. Then cross Great Eastern Road and walk straight down Shoreditch High Street to the bus stop. Take bus 22, 48, 67, or 149 up Kingsland Road.

The Geffrye Museum will be on the right as you go up Kingsland Road. It is in a row of Georgian houses set back from the road with a brick wall and iron railings in front of it. Get off the bus at the stop just after passing it.

13.30 The Geffrye Museum

The Geffrye Museum was originally almhouses built in 1715 by the Ironmonger's Company for widows of its members. The houses were bought in 1910 by the London County Council, and on the request of a number of well-known people they were turned into a furniture museum for students. The museum is now run by the Inner London Education Authority.

The first room you enter is the **Georgian Street** containing shopfronts and doorways. You will also see a woodworker's shop with typical tools used at that time. Behind the woodworker's shop is the kitchen with pewter plates, irons and a wooden mouse-trap.

The next room is the **Elizabethan Room**, with a very ornate fireplace and wooden panelling on the walls to keep the cold out. There are carved chests in which people kept valuables and clothes before chests of drawers were invented.

In the **Stuart and Cromwellian Room** you can see a portrait of Cromwell (1599–1658) and also of Nell Gwynne (1650–87), a favourite of Charles II (1630–85). Be sure to notice the ornate plaster ceiling.

In the **William and Mary Room**, there are replicas of two sash windows with folding shutters. Notice the dog bowl which is emptied through a hole in the side, and the little spinet piano.

You will now pass through the **Chapel** and the **Reference Library**, which are part of the original almshouses. The pine panelling in the Library came from a house in the Strand which was once used by Messrs Coutts, the bankers.

The **Early and Late Georgian Rooms** are pine-panelled but painted in a light colour and are very different from the dark wood of the other rooms. The furniture is in the style of Thomas Chippendale (1718–79).

In the **Regency Room**, there is a small sofa which

is thought to be either for a child or made by a student. The white marble fireplace dates from 1812.

The **Victorian Room** is much plusher and heavier, and contains lots of knick-knacks including a spitoon for the gentlemen.

There is an early telephone and an electric fire in the **Edwardian Room**.

Before going upstairs to the 1930s rooms, you will go through a collection of hats, shoes and dresses.

15.00 When you come out of the museum go left, walk to the first bus stop, and take a No. 22 bus. Get off the bus at the fourth stop after the rail bridge. From here you can take a No. 5 bus to Old Street Underground, which is the nearest underground station.

If you are not too tired now, you may want to visit Bunhill Burial Fields, the remaining part of one of the oldest cemeteries in London.

15.30 Bunhill Burial Fields

When you get off the bus at Old Street Underground, go left on City Road, and cross the street. You will see an entrance to Bunhill Burial Fields a short distance down City Road.

Bunhill (Bone Hill) was a well-known burial site even before the 1500s, when St Paul's began to send old bones from the churchyard as space was needed to bury people. Between 1665 and 1852, approximately 120,000 were buried here. Although much of the land has been built on, you can still see the graves of Daniel Defoe (1660–1731), who wrote *Robinson Crusoe*, John Bunyan (1628–88), whose most famous work is *Pilgrim's Progress*, and William Blake (1757–1827), the poet and painter.

Did You Spot?
1. The years between which the Powell dolls were dressed?
2. What the three-way picture hanging in the Library shows?
3. What musical instrument is in the Regency Room as well as the pianoforte?

Do You Know?
4. Which material was the oldest and cheapest for making dolls?
5. Which country many of the wooden dolls came from?
6. The names of some of the materials dolls can be made of?
7. What were the earliest toys of metal?
8. The name of the Queen who gave some model rooms to the museum?
9. How rushnips were made?
10. What the wooden lady standing in the William and Mary Room was used for?

TOUR 7
The Tombs of Westminster Abbey

1 St Margaret's Church, Westminster, London SW1.
⊖ Westminster, St James's; Bus 3, 11, 12, 24, 29, 53, 77, 77A, 88, 159

2 Westminster Abbey, Broad Sanctuary, London SW1. Tel. (01) 222 5152
⊖ Westminster, St James's; Bus 3, 11, 12, 24, 29, 53, 77, 77A, 88, 159
Nave and Cloisters: Monday–Tuesday, Thursday–Saturday 08.00–18.00; Wednesday, 08.00–19.45; Sunday, between services
Royal Chapels, Poet's Corner, Choir and Statesmen's Aisle: Monday–Friday 09.00–16.45; Saturday 09.00–14.45 and 15.45–17.45
A ££, S £, under 16s and Ps £; Wheelchair/Shop/Food/Toilet
Norman Undercroft Museum: 10.30–16.30; A £, C £, P £
Chapter House: 16 March–15 October 09.30–18.00; 16 October–15 March 09.30–16.00; A £, C £, P £

3 The Jewel Tower, Old Palace Yard, London SW1. Tel. (01) 222 2219
⊖ Westminster; Bus 3, 12, 53, 77, 77A, 88, 159
15 March–15 October 09.30–18.30; 16 October–14 March 09.30–16.00
Closed: Sunday, 24, 25, 26 December, 1 January
Shop

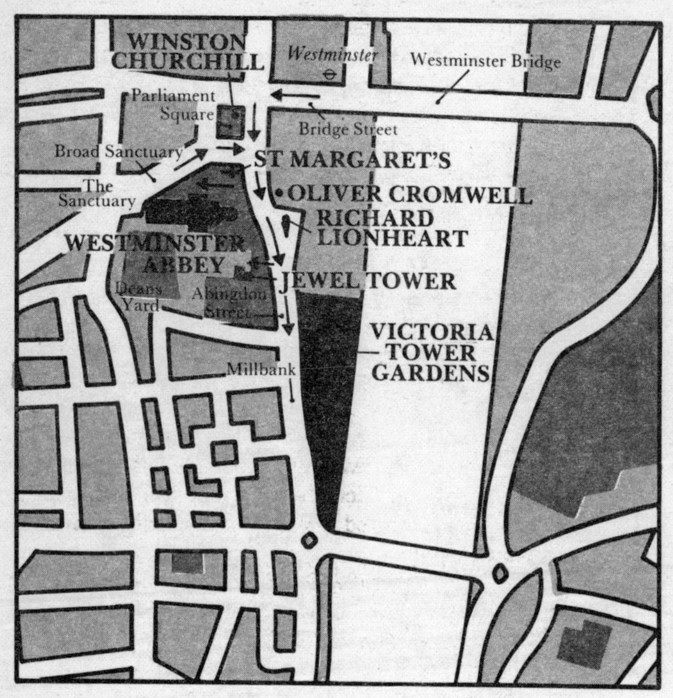

WINSTON CHURCHILL
Westminster
Westminster Bridge
Parliament Square
Bridge Street
Broad Sanctuary
ST MARGARET'S
The Sanctuary
OLIVER CROMWELL
RICHARD LIONHEART
WESTMINSTER ABBEY
JEWEL TOWER
Deans Yard
Abingdon Street
VICTORIA TOWER GARDENS
Millbank

⊖ Westminster

09.30 Go through the barrier and left into the tunnel. As you turn right you will pass the entrance to the Houses of Parliament. When you reach street level, go straight down Bridge Street. Turn with the flow of traffic, noticing the statue of Winston Churchill (1874–1965) on your right. Big Ben is to your left.

As you approach the pedestrian crossing, you will see a statue of Oliver Cromwell (1599–1658) on your left. Cross, turn to your left and enter the east door of St Margaret's Church.

09.45 St Margaret's Church
As you enter the church, you will see a memorial to Sir Walter Raleigh (1554–1618) on your right. He stood trial for treason in 1603, but did not receive the death sentence and was imprisoned in the Tower of London. In 1616, King James I (1566–1625) allowed Raleigh to leave the Tower to explore for gold in South America. He was unsuccessful and, when he returned empty-handed, he received the death sentence. He was executed in Old Palace Yard and buried beneath the altar.

William Caxton (1422–91), the first English printer, is buried in the churchyard. Samuel Pepys (1633–1703) and Winston Churchill were both married here.

Leave St Margaret's by the main doors, go into the square and walk to the west door of the Abbey. Notice the rose window high up being supported by the flying buttresses. As you near the west door, the building you see is Dean's Yard.

10.15 Westminster Abbey
Like many other churches in England, Westminster Abbey was built on the site of an earlier Saxon

Church. In about 1050, Edward the Confessor (1003–66) began a chapel for a Benedictine monastery because he couldn't fulfil a vow to make a pilgrimage to St Peter's in Rome. He also planned to make it his burial place. It was consecrated on 28 December 1065 and Edward died a few days later in 1066. He was buried before the High Altar.

The building as it exists today, however, was mainly built by King Henry III (1207–72). He demolished the eastern part of Edward's chapel and built his church around the remainder. Until the reign of Henry VIII (1491–1547) it was the place of royal marriages, coronations and funerals. Fortunately it did not suffer the fate of other monasteries; it was too important and, for that reason, a Dean was appointed.

The Abbey contains monuments and tombs of many famous, important and interesting people. Many of the tombs are plain stone, but the older ones, up until the 1700s, were painted in bright colours. On some, all the colour is still there, while on others you just see traces of it. But use your imagination and picture how colourful the inside of Westminster Abbey must have been in Queen Elizabeth's reign. On the tombs in the Royal Chapel, there were jewels and gold, which has been stripped off over the years.

The Nave, North and South Transepts

As you enter, you will see a painting of Richard II (1367–1400), who became King in 1377 at the age of 10. Shortly after he was crowned, he put down a rebellion of serfs gathered on the fields across from the Tower of London. He is buried in the Royal Chapel and lies next to his queen, Anne of Bohemia (1366–94).

You will see a bust of Dr Thomas Arnold (1795–1842), Headmaster of Rugby School. Charles Darwin (b. 1809), the author of *The Origin of Species*, was buried here in 1882. Ben Jonson (1574–1637),

Westminster Abbey

the dramatist and poet, was buried standing up, as he was too poor to be buried properly. There is a plaque to Franklin Delano Roosevelt (1882–1941), one of the Presidents of the United States. Near St George's Chapel you will see a stone in the floor commemorating Robert, 1st Baron Baden-Powell (1857–1941).

David Livingstone (1813–73), the African explorer-missionary, was buried here eleven months after he died in Africa. His servants carried his body to Zanzibar, where it was sent to England. There is a large monument against the Choir Screen for Sir Isaac Newton (1642–1727), the famous philosopher and mathematician.

There is a memorial to Sir Stamford Raffles (1781–1826), founder of the colony of Hong Kong and a founding member of the London Zoological Society. There is also one to William Wilberforce (1759–1833), the man who worked so hard to rid the world of slavery.

In **Statesmen's Corner**, you will find William Pitt the Younger (1759–1806), who became Prime Minister at the age of 24 and remained Prime Minister for the rest of his life, except for three years; Sir Robert Peel (1788–1850), twice Prime Minister, who died after falling off his horse on Constitution Hill in Green Park; Benjamin Disraeli (1804–81), a famous Conservative Prime Minister, who influenced Queen Victoria (1819–1901) to take the title of Empress of India; and William Gladstone (1809–98), leader of the Liberal Party and four times Prime Minister.

In **Poet's Corner**, there is a bust of the American poet Henry Wadsworth Longfellow (1807–82). Alfred Tennyson (1809–92) and Robert Browning (1812–89), two Victorian poets, are buried here. You will also see the tomb of the medieval poet Geoffrey Chaucer (1343–1400) against the wall. Chaucer only had a plaque to denote where he was buried until 1555, when he was given a tomb.

There are memorials to John Keats (1795–1821), Percy Bysshe Shelley (1792–1822), William Shakespeare (1564–1616), Robert Burns (1759–96), the three Brontë sisters – Charlotte (1816–55), Emily (1818–48) and Anne (1820–49) – Sir Walter Scott (1771–1832), George Frederick Handel (1685–1759), the composer of 'The Messiah', William Makepeace Thackeray (1811–63), David Garrick (1716–79), actor and friend of Dr Samuel Johnson (1709–84), Charles Dickens (1812–70), and Rudyard Kipling (1865–1936). Against the wall of the Sanctuary is the tomb of Anne of Cleves (1515–57), fourth wife of Henry VIII.

Royal Chapels
As you walk towards the Tomb of Edward the Confessor, you will pass on your right some of the oldest tombs in the Abbey – those of Aymer de Valence (1270–1324), Earl of Pembroke and cousin to Edward I; Edmund Crouchback (1245–96), son of Henry III; and Edward I (1239–1307), son of Henry III, and called the English Justinian because of his parliamentary reforms against the barons.

On your left, you will see the Chapel of our Lady of the Pew, which dates from about 1350, leading to St John's Chapel.

Edward the Confessor Chapel
The tomb or shrine of Edward the Confessor was built for him by William the Conqueror. It sparkled with gold and jewels and had eleven small gold images of kings and saints, but alas these are gone. The recesses in the shrine are places where sick people would be left during the night in the hope that the Saint would cure them.

In this chapel you will find the tombs of Henry III (1207–72), who ruled for 56 years and built the major part of the Abbey as you see it today, and Eleanor of Castile (d. 1290), wife of Edward I. She died in Nottingham and King Edward had crosses built at each place her body lay for the night on the trip to Westminster Abbey.

The tomb of Henry V (1388–1422), who died in France, is here. His embalmed body lay for a time in Rouen Cathedral, and was then laid on an open chariot drawn by four horses and the journey began to England. The clergy, his household and the nobility, then his Queen, Catherine of Valois (1401–1437), followed.

Edward III (1312–77) and Philippa of Hainault (1314–69), his wife, are also buried in this chapel. Philippa was a great influence on Edward III during their long marriage of 42 years. Around the sides of Edward III's tomb were small statues of their fourteen children; only six are left. Richard II and his wife, Anne of Bohemia, are buried here as well.

Don't miss the Coronation Chair with the famous Stone of Scone underneath the seat. Edward I seized the stone from the Scots in 1207 and inserted it in the chair which he had made.

Henry VII's Chapel
The screen around Henry VII's tomb was taken down during the bombing of London in World War II. If you look carefully, you will see where some plates are missing. The tomb itself had a barrier of sandbags put around it.

You will also see the tombs of Queen Elizabeth I (1533–1603), whose crown has disappeared, with her half-sister, Mary I (1516–58); Queen Anne of Denmark (1574–1619), the wife of James I; Mary Queen of Scots (1542–87), who was finally beheaded on the orders of Queen Elizabeth I because of her continual plotting against her; and George II (1683–1760). The only son of Henry VIII, Edward VI (1537–53), is buried under the altar.

12.00　Now visit the **Cloisters** and imagine how they would have appeared with hooded monks walking with their hands folded, heads bowed, rush lamps in brackets on the wall, and the sounds of chanting. You can do some brass rubbings in here of old engraved brasses which were inset into the floors of churches.

You can go into the **Undercroft** and **Abbey Museum**, which is very interesting as it contains death effigies covering about 400 years. A long time ago, when someone died, an effigy would be made to rest on top of the hearse, and after burial it would be placed on top of the tomb and could remain there for many years. The wax effigies are extremely lifelike.

If you want to go into the **Chapter House** you must put special cloth covers on your shoes, because the floor is very old and must not be damaged. The House was built between 1250 and 1253; you will see some old wall paintings that have been uncovered.

After early mass, 80 monks gathered here every day, sat round the walls on stone benches while discussing the business of running the monastery, and received orders from the Abbot on their daily duties. From the reign of Edward I to that of Henry VIII, the Chapter House was used as a Parliament House for the Commons.

Below the Chapter House is the place where the jewels of the King were stored. During Edward I's reign the treasury was broken into and the Crown Jewels and money were stolen. The Abbot and 48 monks were sent to the Tower and two were convicted. The jewels were transferred to the Tower for safekeeping.

13.00 You can buy something to eat in Dean's Yard in the summer, but expect queues between 12.00 and 14.00.

When you leave the Abbey walk back and cross to the Houses of Parliament. Turn right, walking past a statue of Richard the Lionheart (1157–99) on the left. Walk to Victoria Tower Gardens, which is a very nice place to eat a packed lunch. Then cross Millbank and turn right, walking until you see the Jewel Tower on your left. Go down the steps to reach it.

14.00　The Jewel Tower

This tower was built in 1365 for Edward III to hold his jewels and valuable vessels. It was used until Henry VIII's death. There is a pieced-together table support and a drawing showing how the table would have looked. It is thought to have been a part of the high table at Westminster Hall at which royalty would have sat.

Your closest underground station is Westminster.

Did You Spot?

1. The tomb of the Unknown Soldier?
2. A man leaning backwards with music under his arm?
3. The tomb depicting the murder of Thomas Thynne? What is he riding in?

Do You Know?

4. What book was written about Rugby School and Dr Arnold?
5. What Henry Stanley said to Dr Livingstone when he finally found him?
6. What movement was founded by Baden-Powell?
7. Whose effigy is in a naval uniform?
8. Who was President of the United States during World War II?
9. What leaf Sir Walter Raleigh bought back from a voyage?
10. What a long march to the Middle East was called in the Middle Ages?

TOUR 8
Famous Faces

1 The National Portrait Gallery, St Martin's
Place, London WC2. Tel. (01) 930 1552
⊖ Charing Cross, Leicester Square; Bus 3, 6, 11, 12, 23,
24, 29, 53, 77, 77A, 88, 159
10.00–17.00 Monday–Friday; 10.00–18.00 Saturday;
14.00–18.00 Sunday
Closed: 1st Monday May, Good Friday,
24, 25, 26 December, 1 January
Wheelchair/Shop/Toilet

2 Banqueting House, Whitehall, London SW1. Tel.
(01) 930 4179
⊖ Charing Cross, Embankment, Westminster; Bus 3, 11,
12, 24, 29, 53, 77, 88, 159
10.00–17.00 Tuesday–Saturday; 14.00–17.00 Sunday
Closed: Monday, Good Friday, 24, 25, 26 December,
1 January; at short notice for Government functions.
A £, C £, P £, Under 5 Free; Shop

Special Events
Beating the Retreat, Horseguards Parade
1st week June, Tuesday, 18.30, Wednesday and Thursday,
21.30
**Trooping the Colour for the Queen's Official
Birthday,** Horseguards
1st or 2nd Saturday of June, depending on the Queen's
calendar. At 10.00 guards begin to assemble at
Buckingham Palace. The Queen leaves the Palace for
Horseguards at 10.45 and returns to the Palace at 12.15;
she goes onto the balcony at about 13.00.

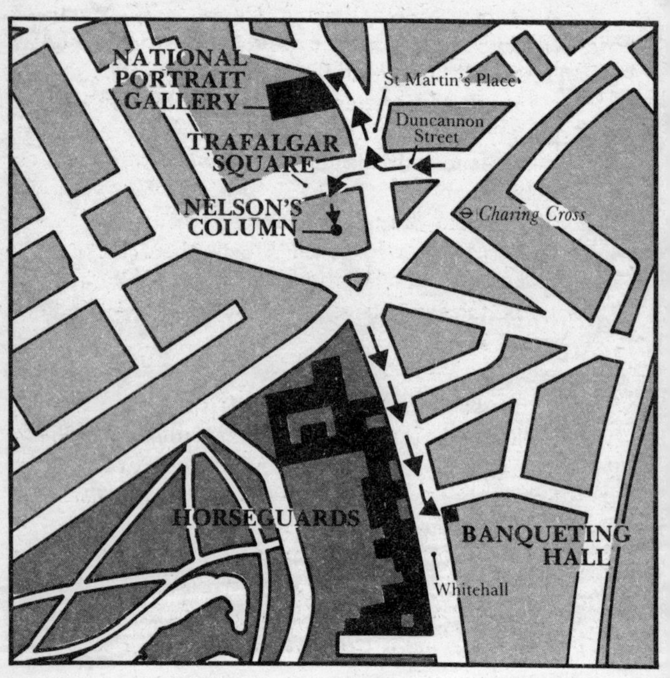

NATIONAL
PORTRAIT
GALLERY
St Martin's Place
Duncannon
Street
TRAFALGAR
SQUARE
Charing Cross
NELSON'S
COLUMN
HORSEGUARDS
BANQUETING
HALL
Whitehall

⊖ Charing Cross

At Charing Cross Underground, go to the right after passing through the barrier and out of the exit for Trafalgar Square. Veer right and go up the stairs.

At street level Charing Cross Station will be directly behind you. You can see the Eleanor Cross (reconstruction), built by Edward I (1239–1307) to mark each place the body of his wife, Eleanor of Castile (1246–90), rested at night on the way to Westminster Abbey for her funeral. Twelve crosses were made.

Go straight down Duncannon Street, cross to the church of St Martin in the Fields, then cross to the left side of St Martin's Place and proceed right. You will find the entrance to the National Portrait Gallery on your left.

10.30 The National Portrait Gallery

The National Portrait Gallery was founded in 1856 to house portraits of famous British men and women – authors, Kings and Queens, artists, politicians, scientists, athletes, etc.

Go up the stairs where you will see a portrait of Lawrence of Arabia (T. E. Lawrence, 1888–1935). Lawrence wrote *The Seven Pillars of Wisdom*, which described his many exploits in the Middle East in the first part of the 1900s.

There is a revolving screen (you will see them throughout the Museum) where changing sides show you photographs or paintings of people. There is a painting of Sir Oswald Mosley (1896–1980), who established the British Union of Fascists and caused many problems in the East End of London; he was finally interned in 1940 until the end of the war. There is a painting of Edward, Duke of Windsor (1894–1972), who, as Edward VIII, gave up the throne to marry Mrs Simpson; he was the brother of the present Queen's father, George VI.

There are revolving screens of scientists and people in the arts – Samuel Beckett (1906–), author of *Waiting for Godot*; Sir Alec Guinness (1914–), actor in many famous films, including *Kind Hearts and Coronets* and *Bridge on the River Kwai*; and James Joyce (1882–1941), who wrote *Finnegan's Wake*.

There is a little room full of photos of Charles Chaplin (1889–1977). You will see a very good painting of Lord Montgomery (1887–1976), the British Field Marshal who was in charge of the 8th Army in Africa. The Beatles and Elton John are also here.

Go out to the area where the information desk is and up the stairs. At the top are portraits of the present Royal Family: The Queen Mother, Prince Charles, Prince Andrew, George VI (1895–1952), Princess Diana, Queen Elizabeth and Prince Philip.

Go up the stairs again where you will see a painting of George V (1865–1936) and Queen Mary (1867–1953) in Buckingham Palace.

Go right into **Room 24** where you will find many Edwardians (the reign of Edward VII, 1841–1910): Robert Louis Stevenson (1850–94), who wrote *Treasure Island*, and Oscar Wilde (1854–1900), the dramatist and poet who was very popular during the late 1800s because of his charm and wit; he wrote *The Picture of Dorian Gray*. You will also see James McNeill Whistler (1834–1903), the American-born painter who lived for many years in Chelsea; his best-known painting is 'Whistler's Mother'.

In the **Hallway** are Robert Baden-Powell (1859–1941), founder of the Boy Scout Movement, and General Gordon (1833–85), who was sent to the Sudan in 1884 to evacuate Europeans and Egyptians from the dangers of the revolt by the Mahdi. He was besieged at Khartoum for ten months and was murdered when the Mahdi overran the fort; relief arrived

Oscar Wilde, after the painting by
Carlo Pellegrini, 1884, in the National
Portrait Gallery

two days later. There is a statue of a woman who first became famous because of her fight to improve the hospital conditions of wounded soldiers in the Crimean War.

You will see a statue of Queen Victoria (1819–1901) and Prince Albert (1819–61), and in the room next to it you will see paintings of Queen Victoria's reign. You can see the Brontë sisters, painted by their brother Branwell (1817–48). On the left is Anne (1820–49), who wrote *Agnes Gray*, then Emily (1818–48), who wrote *Wuthering Heights*, and finally Charlotte (1816–55), who wrote *Jane Eyre*. There is also a portrait of Charles Dickens (1812–70), the most famous author of the 1800s.

Walk back and into **Room 20**. You will see Robert Stevenson (1803–59), who built the engine called the Rocket, with his father, George. There is Isambard Kingdom Brunel (1806–59), who is considered to be one of the most original inventors of the 1800s; he designed the Clifton suspension bridge over the Avon Gorge and the first screw propeller ships. You will also see Charles Darwin (1809–82), whose theories about the origin of humans caused such a sensation in the last century.

In **Room 21**, you can see Dante Gabriel Rossetti (1828–82), painter-poet, who opened his wife's grave in Highgate Cemetery several years after her death in order to retrieve poems he had written. You can also see his sister, Christina Georgina (1830–74), who was also a poet, and his mother. There is Elizabeth Barrett Browning (1806–61), famous for *Sonnets from the Portuguese*, Julia Margaret Cameron (1815–79), who is known for her photographs, and George Eliot (1819–80), who changed her name from Mary Ann Evans in order to be more acceptable as an author in the days when men thought women couldn't write. The Brontë sisters did this as well.

Go back to the central area and up the stairs.

Above you are effigies from the tombs of Edward III (1312–77), Richard II (1367–1400), his wife, Anne of Bohemia (1366–1400), and Edward, the Black Prince (1330–76), son of Edward III.

There is a copy of the painting in Westminster Abbey of Richard II, and one of Geoffrey Chaucer (1342–1400), who was in the service of Edward III and Richard II. Chaucer was one of the first authors to begin writing in English as it was spoken then, as opposed to Latin or French.

The walls here are covered with all the paintings of queens and kings which appear in the guidebooks: Richard III (1452–85), about whom there is still argument waged as to whether or not he had his two nephews killed in the Tower; Henry V (1387–1422), the hero of the Battle of Agincourt (1415); and Henry VIII (1491–1547), the man known for his number of wives, the way he rid himself of them and his break with the Catholic Church. There is the family of Thomas More (1477–1535), a copy of the painting by Hans Holbein (1497–1543). More was a lawyer at Lincoln's Inn, a friend of Henry VIII and on the Privy Council. He became Chancellor when Wolsey was deposed but resigned as he would not accept Henry VIII becoming head of the English church. He was tried for treason, defending himself brilliantly, but was convicted on false evidence and beheaded.

In the **Elizabeth I Room**, you can see Sir Walter Raleigh (1552–1618), who was imprisoned in the Tower for many years and who, while there, wrote the *History of the World*. He was beheaded after an unsuccessful search for gold in South America. He was responsible for bringing the potato and tobacco to England.

There is William Shakespeare (1564–1616), born at Stratford-upon-Avon, whose plays are still acted today all over the world and influence many different cultures. Who hasn't heard of Hamlet, Puck, Macbeth, and Romeo and Juliet?

There is Ben Jonson (1573–1637), who wrote poems
and plays, including *Every Man in His Humour*,
where each person had a particular obsession; John
Donne (1572–1631), a poet, who studied at Oxford
and Lincoln's Inn and was put in prison for secretly
marrying the daughter of a man who helped support
him.

Here is Oliver Cromwell (1599–1658) who, after
deposing Charles I (1600–1649), was made Lord Protector of England; he established Puritanism in
England. Nell Gwynne (1650–87) sold oranges in
Drury Lane, Covent Garden, and then went on to
become a comedy actress whereupon she caught the
eye of Charles II (1630–85). Samuel Pepys
(1633–1703) wrote short-hand diaries from 1660 to
1669 which give descriptions of life during the Plague
and the Great Fire of London.

You can see James II (1633–1701), the second son
of Charles I. He was the brother of Charles II, and
when Charles died he became King. He had become a
Roman Catholic, and although he wanted religious
freedom for all denominations, he faced continual
revolts and was eventually overthrown. His last
attempt to regain the crown was defeated by William
III (1650–1701), Mary II's husband. His two daughters, Mary II (1662–94) and Anne (1665–1714),
became Queens.

There is Isaac Newton (1642–1727), who first discovered the law of gravity while sitting under an
apple tree. He also discovered calculus and recognized
that white light is a mixture of coloured lights.

Go out to the right. You will see Jonathan Swift
(1667–1745), a poet and satirist (criticizes folly or vice
by using scorn or ridicule); the book he is best known
for is *Gulliver's Travels*. There is Christopher Wren
(1632–1723), architect, whose tombstone says with
regard to St Paul's, 'If you seek his monument, look

around,' and Edmund Halley (1656–1742), an astronomer and friend of Isaac Newton, who discovered
that comets have periodic orbits and do not appear
randomly. He also identified a particular comet which
appears every 76 years, and although he predicted its
next arrival he did not live long enough to see it
again.

Go straight into **Room 8**. You can see a painting of
a gaols (prison) enquiry into the Fleet Prison (near
the present Old Bailey), previously used as a debtor's
prison. The enquiry was to determine if warders
tortured prisoners into giving them money.

On the left is Johann Christian Bach (1735–82),
music master to the Royal Family. He was the ele-
venth son of Johann Sebastian Bach (1685–1750),
who had a total of 20 children, three of whom were
famous musicians. William Hogarth (1697–1764),
painter and engraver, is also here – his best-known
works, which are social satires, are 'The Rake's Progress', 'Industry and Idleness' and 'Gin Lane'.

Go straight into **Room 10**. Here is George III
(1738–1820), King of England during the American
War of Independence, and William Pitt ((1783–1801),
who was his Prime Minister.

In **Room 13** are Percy Bysshe Shelley (1792–1822),
the poet who wrote a revolutionary poem called
'Queen Mab' and left soon after for Italy; he died in a
sailing accident. His wife, Mary Wollstonecraft Shelley (1797–1851), wrote the story of *Frankenstein*.
There is Walter Scott (1771–1832), writer of many
historical novels; Robert Burns (1759–96), the Scottish poet, who has admirers all over the world; Edward
Jenner (1749–1823), the physician who discovered the
vaccine against smallpox; and James Watt
(1736–1819), the engineer whose work on steam
engines made him one of the most important contribu-
tors to the industrial revolution.

In **Room 15** are George IV (1762–1830), who was

not a popular King, being satirized for his insatiable appetite and extravagant life-style, and William IV (1765–1837), known as Silly Billy, who was succeeded by his niece, Victoria, because his two daughters died in infancy. In this room you will see cases with miniature paintings – lift up the covers to see them: there is one of Jane Austen (1775–1817), whose ironic wit is so beautifully illustrated in the character of Mr Collins, the vicar, in *Pride and Prejudice*, and Jeremy Bentham (1748–1832), a philosopher who went to Lincoln's Inn to study law when he was 15. He supported the founding of University College, London, and bequeathed his body to the University. His head is now in a box, in a safe, and his body with a wax head sits in a tall box with a door in one of the corridors of the University.

Now go back through Rooms 14 and 13 to the stairs down.

12.00 Trafalgar Square

When you leave the Gallery, go over to Trafalgar Square, where you can sit and eat your lunch or just rest your feet. See how many pigeons you can have sitting on your head or on your arm, while holding the food in your hand. Climb the lions and dangle your feet in the fountains.

Notice Nelson's Column, which was built in 1842. The square is named after the Battle of Trafalgar (21 October 1805) in which Nelson defeated the French navy, but was unfortunately killed.

The statue of Charles I faces the Banqueting House, from which he walked to his execution on 30 January 1649. This statue was made in 1633 while he was still alive.

Leave Trafalgar Square by crossing at the lights at the south-east corner. Go down the subway and walk through the underground station and out the other end. Have a look at Admiralty Arch, which leads to the Mall and to Buckingham Palace.

Go down Whitehall to Horseguards, which is on your right.

13.00 Horseguards

This Horseguards building was built in 1750 and once housed the offices of the Commander in Chief of the Army. When the Duke of Wellington was Commander in Chief, his offices were above the archway.

The archway from Whitehall is the official entrance to Buckingham Palace and is therefore guarded by the Queen's Household Cavalry, comprised of the Life Guards and the Blues and Royals who guard in alternate months. The Life Guards have uniforms of white trousers, red jacket and white plume. The Blues and Royals have white trousers, blue jacket and red plumes.

You will find the guards in the sentry boxes on duty from 10.00 to 16.00, changing at 11.00. After 16.00 there are dismounted guards on sentry duty under the arch.

Walk through the arch. The St James's Park side of Horseguards is where Henry VIII had his tilting yard, which existed through Elizabeth's reign, and was then used for parade practice. This is where the Trooping of the Colour occurs.

Walk back to Whitehall and cross the road. The Banqueting House is on the corner of Horseguards Avenue and Whitehall.

Banqueting House

This was built for James I in 1619, and Charles I commissioned Peter Paul Rubens (1577–1640) to paint the ceiling; he walked to the scaffold through a

window where the stairs are now. The House was
built for entertainments such as masques (a dramatic
court entertainment using verse, dance and music)
and balls, but has had various other uses, including
that of a Royal Chapel.

When you leave the Banqueting House, walk back up
Whitehall to Trafalgar Square. Cross round to your
right until you reach the underground station.

Did You Spot?
1. The famous actor as you first went up the stairs?
2. A famous sprinter?
3. The famous lady who was in the Crimea? Who was she?
4. What was strange about the family painting of Thomas
    More?

Do You Know?
5. The names of two sisters in the painting on the left
    where the Royal portraits are?
6. Who Sir Walter Raleigh spread his cloak on the ground
    for?
7. A nickname of William Shakespeare which relates to
    him being a poet?
8. What Isaac Newton was?
9. What the comet which appears every 76 years is called?
10. What happens when you use the box on wheels in the
    Banqueting House?

TOUR 9
The Sea, Time and the Heavens:
A Day at Greenwich

1 Thames Boats, Westminster Pier, London SW1.
Tel. (01) 930 0971
⚙ Westminster
Booking office opens at 10.00 and boats leave every 30
minutes from 10.30 A ££, C ££ Return

**2, 3 The National Maritime Museum and The
Old Royal Observatory,** Greenwich, London
SE10.
Tel. (01) 858 4422
Boat Greenwich Pier; Train BR to Greenwich Station
Bus 108B, 177, 180, 185, 188
Summer: 10.00–18.00 Monday–Saturday; 14.00–17.30
Sunday
Winter: 10.00–17.00 Monday–Friday; 10.00–17.30 Saturday;
14.00–17.00 Sunday
A ££, C £, P £, S £; Part Wheelchair/Shop/Food/Toilet

4 Cutty Sark, Greenwich, London SE10.
Tel. (01) 853 3589
Boat Greenwich Pier; Train BR to Greenwich Station
Bus 108B, 177, 180, 185, 188
Easter to 30 September: 10.30–18.00 Monday–Saturday;
14.30–18.00 Sunday
1 October to Easter: 10.30–17.00 Monday–Saturday;
14.30–17.00 Sunday 14.30–18.00 Good Friday
A £, C £, P £, S £; Wheelchair/Shop

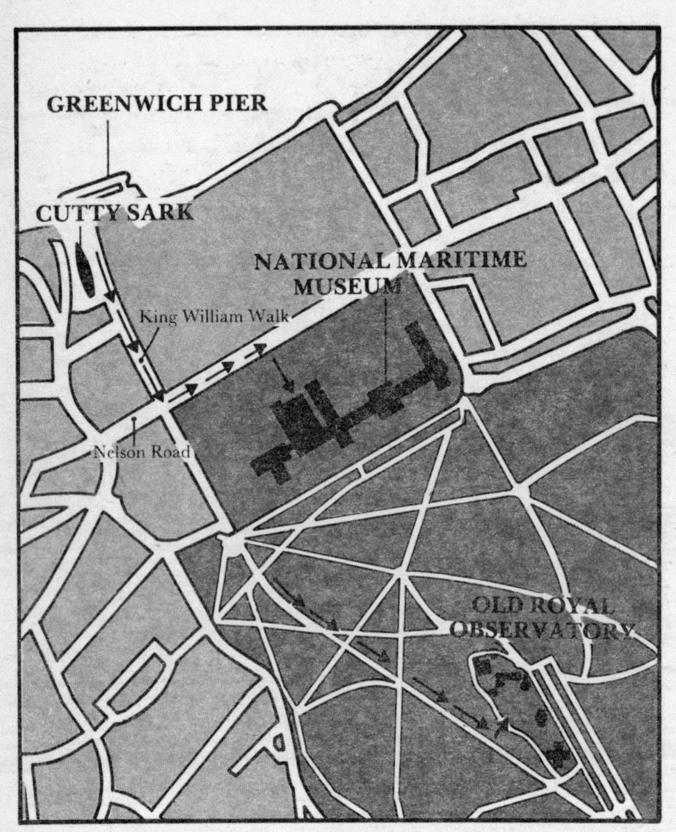

GREENWICH PIER
CUTTY SARK
NATIONAL MARITIME MUSEUM
King William Walk
Nelson Road
OLD ROYAL OBSERVATORY

⊖ Westminster

10.00 Try to arrive early enough for one of the first boats to Greenwich. It is a very popular place and also you may want to spend more time than you have planned for in the Museum, as it is chock-a-block with interesting things to see.

When you come out of Westminster Underground, go down the subway steps and turn left. This takes you directly to the boats.

10.30 Thames Boats

The Thames is a tidal river and has a long tradition of use for commerce, transport and pleasure. The Romans built their bridge near where London Bridge is today.

You will see many landmarks of London as you ride down the Thames towards Greenwich. You will pass Festival Hall, St Paul's, The Monument, the Tower of London, London Bridge, etc.

11.15 When you get to Greenwich, walk past the *Cutty Sark* and straight up King William Road. When you reach the intersection with Nelson and Romney Roads, cross and turn left. The entrance to the Museum is on the right a short distance up this road.

As you walk along the side of the Museum, you can see Greenwich Park stretching up the hill and the red ball on top of Flamsteed House. This ball drops punctually at 13.00 hrs GMT, as it has since 1833, as a time check for passing ships.

11.30 The National Maritime Museum

When you enter the Museum, go up the stairs. You will pass Queen Anne's astronomical clock as you enter an area which has changing exhibitions. Go in the direction of Galleries 14–24.

After you have finished looking at the exhibitions go down the stairs.

There you will see a model of Captain James Cook's (1728–79) ship *Discovery* and models of all the crew and cargo needed to sail it. You can see a French guillotine blade captured in 1794 at Guadeloupe and small globes of the world.

Horatio Nelson's (1758–1805) body lay in state in the Painted Hall at Greenwich. On the day of his funeral his body was placed on an open boat for a procession by river to St Paul's. It was a very stormy day – the river was high and there were choppy waves – and many people lined the bank to watch the procession.

Have a look at the figurehead which was on the carriage which took Nelson's body from the Thames to St Paul's Cathedral. The carriage is shown in a drawing in the glass cabinet. There is also the pigtail of Nelson, which was cut off at his instruction as he lay dying for presentation to Lady Emma Hamilton (1761–1815). There are several paintings of Napoleon (1769–1821). Below, you can see the ship *Cornwallis*.

When you finish looking at the exhibits on this floor, leave by the exit which takes you to the entrance of the Museum. Then go down the ramp. This takes you into the **Archaeology Section**.

You will see exhibits of parts of several ancient barges – one from the Bronze Age, found in North Ferriby in the Humber River, and a 10th Century one found at Graveney. Walk past the *Cornwallis*, out through the doors and into the entrance again.

Now go down the steps to the right under the figure of Queen Charlotte, which was on the Royal Yacht you are about to see. Go into the **Neptune Hall** and have a look at the steam ship *Reliant* and a beautiful steam yacht. Along the walls you can see carved figureheads. When you have finished looking at the *Reliant*, go into the **Barge House**.

Lion figurehead, *c.* 1715, from the
National Maritime Museum

Here you will find the golden barge (1732) of Frederick, the eldest son of George II (1683–1760). The first time this barge was used, Frederick and wife went down river to see how the cleaning of paintings was proceeding. Imagine the barge on the River Thames, with lords and ladies following, and a boat full of musicians following them. You will also see Queen Mary's (1662–95) shallop, built in 1689. A shallop is a small open boat fitted with oars or sails, or both.

13.00 Come out of the Museum and turn right so that you are walking behind the Museum. As you near the end you will see a coffee house/restaurant to the side. You can eat here quite reasonably or buy sandwiches to eat in the Park.

To the left of the coffee house is a gate into Greenwich Park. Walk up the hill to the Old Royal Observatory.

Just before you turn into the grounds of the Observatory, you will see the electrical 24-hour clock built in 1852, which chimes every hour. These are the chimes heard on the BBC radio broadcasts.

14.00 **The Old Royal Observatory**

In 1675 King Charles II (1630–85) ordered that a Royal Observatory be built at Greenwich to study the problems of longitude with regard to navigation; the first astronomer, John Flamsteed (1646–1719), moved in a year later. He made a very precise 3000-star catalogue.

Walk across the courtyard and notice the straight brass line running through the cobbles. This is the world's Prime Meridian, longitude zero. It runs from North to South poles.

At the time the Observatory was built, zero longitude could be placed anywhere a map maker or chart maker wished. This affected navigation and time (there was a difference of 15 minutes between London and Plymouth). By the middle of the 1700s the Greenwich reading was being used more and more, and finally, in 1884, it was chosen as the Prime Meridian longitude zero reading.

You will also see the tombstone of Edmund Halley (1656–1742) and some members of his family. He discovered that comets have periodic orbits and identified one, which is named after him. He calculated that it would appear every 76 years.

The first floor of Flamsteed House is called the **Octagonal Room** and was used for occasional observations for 150 years. This room has changed little since it was designed by Christopher Wren (1632–1723). Go out through the door marked 'exit', which takes you down into the **Halley Gallery**. You can see the living area arranged as it would have looked in the 1700s.

Leave Flamsteed House and walk over to the **Meridian Building**. Here you will see a scene of Flamsteed's equitorial sextant being used. The principles of sextants were first discovered in 1730, and greatly improved navigation in measuring angular distances. You will see astrolabes, which sailors used in determining latitude before the sextant; ring sundials, which folded flat and told time; globes of the world and sandglass timers.

Walk back the way you came from Greenwich Pier. Be sure to stop at the *Cutty Sark* on your way back.

15.30 **Cutty Sark**

This clipper ship started carrying tea from China in 1870. She next carried wool from Australia and after several owners she was finally presented to the Cutty Sark Society.

There is an exhibition about the life of the ship and you can see where the sailors slept, ate and worked.

16.15 Back on to the Thames for your ride to Westminster
       Pier.

Did You Spot?
  1. The cannons as you walked to the Museum entrance?
     How many were there?
  2. The only non-human figurehead in Neptune's Gallery?

Do You Know?
  3. Where the very small globes of the world were kept
     when not in use?
  4. Where Prince Frederick's barge first went?
  5. What animal Horatio Nelson tracked when he was on
     an expedition to Russia?
  6. Who Queen's House was originally built for?
  7. Which famous Tudor king was born at Greenwich?
  8. Where and when Nelson died?
  9. What a shallop was used for?
 10. Why Captain Cook was famous?

TOUR 10
The Story of London

1 St Mary-le-Bow, Cheapside, London EC2.
⊖ Bank, Mansion House; Bus 501, 25 and others
09.00–18.00 Monday–Friday; *Closed*: Saturday, Sunday,
Bank Holidays

**2 The Priory Church of St Bartholomew the
Great,** West Smithfield, London EC1. Tel. (01) 606 1575
⊖ Barbican, St Paul's; Bus 4, 8, 22, 25, 277, 279
Wheelchair

3 The Museum of London, London Wall,
London EC2. Tel. (01) 600 3699
⊖ Barbican, Moorgate, St Paul's
Bus 4, 141, 279A, 502 to St Paul's; 6, 8, 9, 9A, 11, 15, 22,
25, 501, 513
10.00–18.00 Tuesday–Saturday; 14.00–18.00 Sunday
Wheelchair/Shop/Food/Toilet/Quizzes and Worksheets

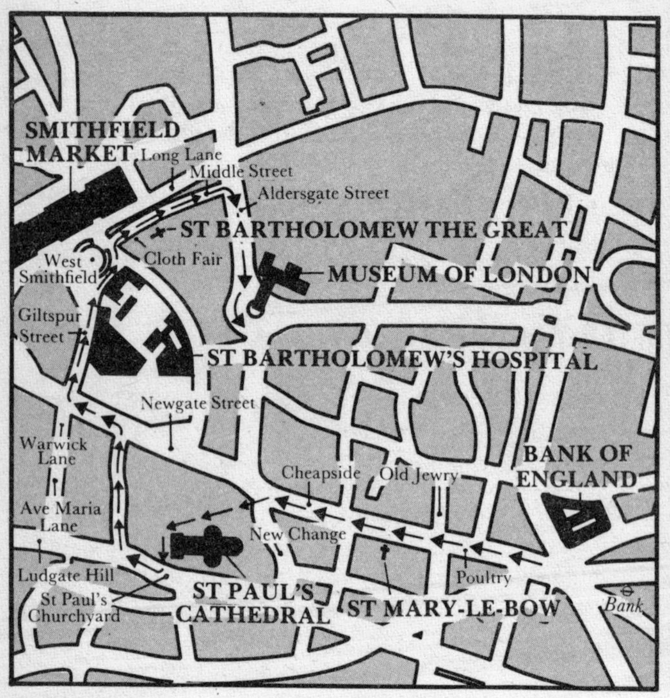

SMITHFIELD MARKET
Long Lane
Middle Street
Aldersgate Street
ST BARTHOLOMEW THE GREAT
West Smithfield
Cloth Fair
MUSEUM OF LONDON
Giltspur Street
ST BARTHOLOMEW'S HOSPITAL
Newgate Street
Warwick Lane
Cheapside
Old Jewry
BANK OF ENGLAND
Ave Maria Lane
New Change
Ludgate Hill
St Paul's Churchyard
ST PAUL'S CATHEDRAL
Poultry
ST MARY-LE-BOW
Bank

⊖ Bank

10.00 The Bank Underground Station is very confusing as it services Northern, Central, Circle and District Lines.

Whatever line you arrive on, exit where it is marked 'Central Line & Waterloo & City Lines'. You will see Cheapside signposted, turn left, and then left again at the arrow to Cheapside. At street level walk down Mansion House Street, which leads to Poultry Street. Poultry Street becomes Cheapside. After you cross Old Jewry Street, cross to the other side. Walk straight down Cheapside to the church of St Mary-le-Bow, which will be on your left.

10.20 **St Mary-le-Bow**

The medieval St Mary-le-Bow was destroyed in the fire of 1666. Christopher Wren (1632–1723) designed the new St Mary-le-Bow as both a church and a meeting house for the people in the area. He wanted something simple and open (no high pews and tombs).

The church was gutted in World War II, but because Christopher Wren's plans for the church were available it was possible to rebuild what had been destroyed. The stained glass is modern, as is the wood.

In the churchyard, you will see a statue of Captain John Smith (1580–1631), the colonizer of Virginia and the man saved from death by the Indian princess Pocahontas (c. 1595–1617).

10.45 Now go left and continue up Cheapside, walking towards St Paul's. When you reach St Paul's walk left round it. St Paul's Cathedral is the most famous architectual design of Christopher Wren. It would be a good idea to buy some sandwiches in this area for eating later.

Go straight into Ludgate Hill. Then turn right into

Ave Maria and continue into Warwick Street. Turn left at Newgate Street. As you reach the junction with the Old Bailey, you will see a sign indicating that the Newgate Prison was on this site until 1777, when the Old Bailey was built. This building does not date from 1777, but was built in 1907. There has been a prison on this site since the Middle Ages.

Cross Newgate Street and go into Giltspur Street. You will pass St Bartholomew's Hospital, which was founded by Rahere (d. 1143) at the same time as he founded Bartholomew the Great. On your left, you will see a statue of the 'fat boy' attached to the corner building on Cock Lane. The statue is from a pub sign, but there are people who think it denotes where the Great Fire stopped.

Still walking up Giltspur Street you will see Smithfield Market in front of you. At the time Rahere acquired this land, there was a horse market here, which changed to a cattle and sheep market in the 1700s. St Bartholomew's Cloth Fairs were held here; it was also the site of jousting tournaments in the reigns of Edward III (1312–77) and King Richard II (1367–1400), who met Wat Tyler and the revolting peasants here in 1381.

Walk round to the right. You will see the original gateway to the priory with a Tudor house built on top. Many Protestant martyrs were burned at the stake in front of this gate on the orders of Queen Mary I (Bloody Mary, 1516–58).

11.30 The Priory Church of St Bartholomew the Great

St Bartholomew the Great originally covered much more land than it does today. Henry VIII (1491–1547) ordered that parts of it be destroyed, as well as the monastery. Luckily, residents of the area resisted his orders and were able to save what you see today, the

Quire. This was the oldest part of the church, built in
1145, and is a good example of a Norman chapel.
After the dissolution, the Quire was used as living
accomodation; later it contained a blacksmith's shop
and a factory for making fringes. Benjamin Franklin
(1706–90) also worked here in a printing works.

12.00 When you leave St Bartholomew, turn right into
Cloth Fair, leading into Middle Street, and then turn
right into Aldersgate Street. You will see the Museum
of London signposted here. When you come to the
roundabout, continue straight on to the stairs leading
to the Museum.

12.30 The Museum of London

The first floor begins with the Story of London from
prehistoric times to 1666, when the fire destroyed
most of the City.

In the Prehistoric Section, look for the flint hand
tools, pottery and bronze axeheads.

In the Roman section, you will see a model of what
a Roman quay would have looked like. There are
pottery, bracelets, slave irons, farming implements,
tombs, inscriptions and many other things. There are
also reconstructions of a Roman kitchen and dining
room.

In the Anglo-Saxon exhibition there is a model of
William the Conqueror's (1028–87) White Tower.

The Tudor exhibition has a beautiful selection of
jewellery and a model of London Bridge.

You can see Oliver Cromwell's (1599–1658) death
mask and learn what happened to his body.

There is a bedroom from a Jacobean House and a
model of the Globe Theatre.

Don't miss the Great Fire exhibition.

Then go down the walkway to the next level where
you will find the exhibitions on London after the fire.

'Twelve pence a peck oysters!'
A London street trader

Here you will see house signs, the garden gate from Christopher Wren's house, a late Stuart interior with a carved fireplace, a virginal, a long-case clock and a sedan chair.

There is a Georgian printing press, the doors from old Newgate Prison with two cells, and a Georgian doll's house.

Look at the early 19th Century model of Crystal Palace from the Great Exhibition of 1851. There are fire-engines, a schoolroom, shop fronts, a Victorian tobacco shop, hairdresser, bank, tailor and grocer.

The 20th Century section contains 1920s furniture and here things are beginning to resemble what we use today.

There are several underground stations which you can use when you finish at the Museum. St Paul's will probably be the easiest and is on the Central Line. The Bank can be used during the week only and is on the Circle Line. Moorgate, on the Northern Line, is difficult to find as it weaves through the Barbican.

Did You Spot?
1. What the Romans wrote letters on?
2. A coach as you went across the walkway? Whose is it?

Do You Know?
3. What Roman soldiers were called?
4. The name of the Roman General who invaded England?
5. What Nursery Rhyme mentions St Mary-le-Bow?
6. What discovery Benjamin Franklin made?
7. Which famous actor-playwright acted in the Globe Theatre in the 1660s?
8. How many churches Christopher Wren designed after the Great Fire?

TOUR 11

Outer Space, Underwater and Inside the Earth

1 The Science Museum, Exhibition Rd, South
Kensington, London SW7. Tel. (01) 589 3456
 South Kensington; Bus 9, 14, 30, 45, 52, 73, 74, 96,
297
10.00–1800 Monday–Saturday; 14.30–18.00 Sunday.
Closed: Good Friday, May Day Monday, 25, 26 December,
1 January
Wheelchair/Shop/Food/Toilet

2 The Geological Museum, Exhibition Rd, South
Kensington, London SW7. Tel. (01) 589 3444
 South Kensington; Bus 9, 14, 30, 45, 52, 73, 74, 96,
297
10.00–1800 Monday–Saturday; 14.30–18.00 Sunday.
Closed: Good Friday, 1st Monday May, 24, 25, 26
December, 1 January
Wheelchair/Shop/Food/Toilet

3 Michael Faraday's Laboratory, The Royal
Institution, 21 Albemarle St, London W1.
Tel. (01) 409 2992
 Green Park, Piccadilly Circus; Bus 14, 19, 22, 25, 38,
55
13.00–16.00 Tuesday and Thursday
A £, C £; Wheelchairs (no toilet)/Toilet

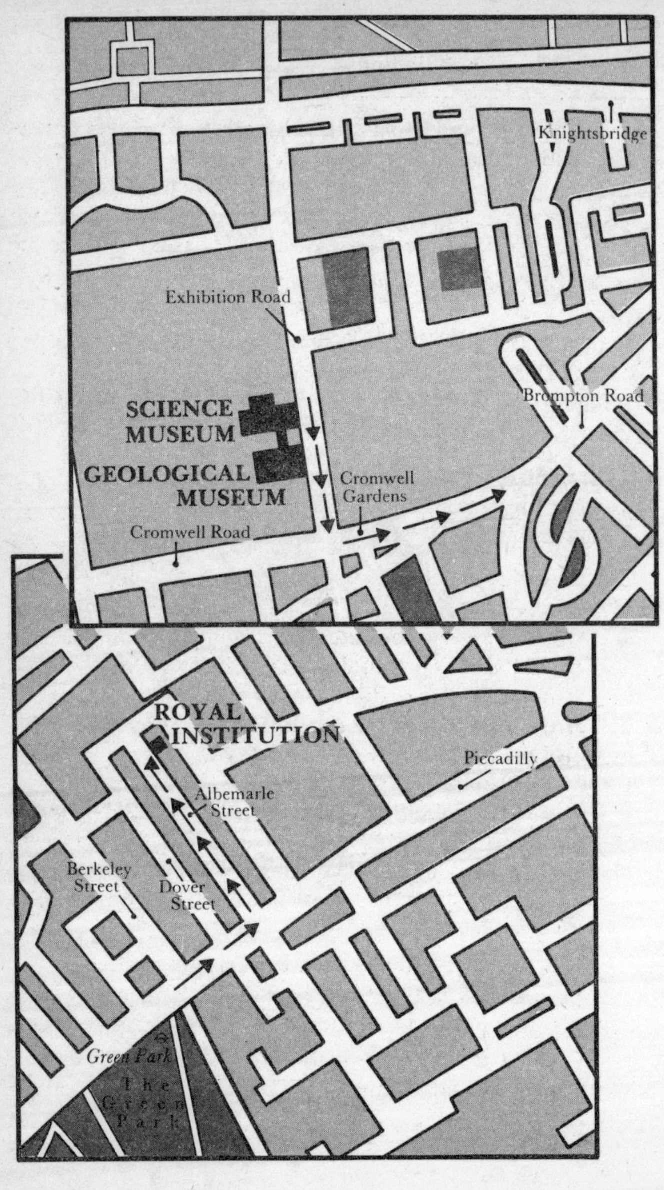

Knightsbridge
Exhibition Road
Brompton Road
SCIENCE MUSEUM
GEOLOGICAL MUSEUM
Cromwell Gardens
Cromwell Road
ROYAL INSTITUTION
Piccadilly
Albemarle Street
Berkeley Street
Dover Street
Green Park
The Green Park

⊖ South Kensington

This tour will be particularly interesting to teenagers with a flair for science. Concentrate on the upper floors of the Science Museum and then go to Michael Faraday's Laboratory at the Royal Institution, which is only open on Tuesday and Thursdays. Skip the Children's Gallery.

With younger children, concentrate on the lower floors of the Science Museum and the Geological Museum.

If you want to see certain exhibits in the Science Museum, it would be best to buy a Museum Guide. The Guide has a very good map of each floor.

10.00 The Science Museum

Follow the signs to the Museums and pass the first exit to the Natural History Museum and the Victoria and Albert Museum. The Science Museum is next.

Go into the **Entrance Hall** and carry on into the main part of the building. To your right you will see a James Watt rotation beam engine of 1788. Next to it is another similar one which can be operated for the benefit of visitors.

Carry on down the hall, past Exploration, into the **Transport Gallery**. Here you will see Puffing Billy, the oldest surviving locomotive in the world. There are many models of old cars, steam engines and a trolley which children will have a good time making work.

If you go downstairs while here you will enter the **Children's Gallery**. All through the Science Museum are working exhibits and this is no exception. Here they can get information on human and animal power, periscopes, internal combustion, air vacuums, light reflection, energy, pulleys.

Also on the lower ground floor is an exhibition of

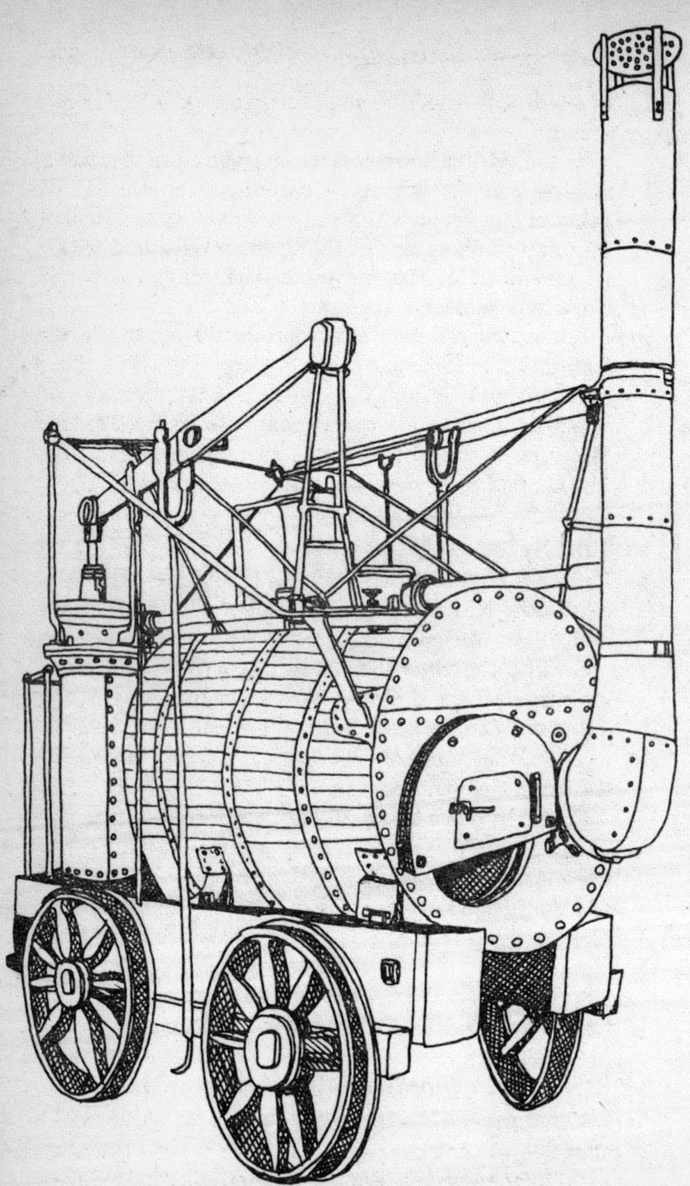

Puffing Billy, from the Science Museum

domestic appliances, including a model of a Victorian kitchen.

On the **First Floor** are astronomical instruments, mapmaking, surveying, time measurement and meteorological instruments.

Carry on to the east side and go into the agricultural implement collection, early textile machinery, hand and machine tools, and exhibitions on the history of glass, iron and steel production and tele-communications.

The **Second Floor** has exhibits on weights and measures, chemistry and lighting, the structure of matter, and printing and paper-making. There are also exhibits on nuclear physics and power, industrial chemistry, pure chemistry, computing, navigation, ships, docks and sea diving.

In a gallery above the Second Floor at the west end are exhibits on docks and diving.

On the **Third Floor** you will find exhibitions of photography and cinematography, optics, talking machines, heat and temperature, early physics, electricity and magnetism, geophysics, and aeronautics.

In the geophysics exhibition are the stairs or lifts to the Wellcome Foundation Medical Exhibition.

The **Fourth Floor** is called 'Glimpses of Medical History' and contains full-sized reconstructions of medical practices from prehistory to modern times.

The **Fifth Floor** has an exhibition called 'The Science and Art of Medicine.'

When you leave the Science Museum, turn right and it is only a few steps to the Geological Museum.

12.00 The Geological Museum

On the **Ground Floor**, you will find very good exhibitions on volcanoes, erosion, the growth of continents, earthquakes and the formation of our earth. There is an earthquake simulator which children will find exciting. To get to the simulator, go up the stairs at the entrance, turn left and go up a further three stairs and then walk straight ahead. There is also a very good exhibition of precious stones.

On the **First Floor**, you will see how England is divided into seventeen areas, and find detailed geological information for each.

On the **Second Floor** are ores, non-metallic minerals, exhibits on oil and coal, and a model of Stonehenge.

1.00 For lunch, there is a McDonald's take-away in the area and a very good cafeteria in the Victoria and Albert Museum. You can sit and eat your lunch on a small slice of land across from the Victoria and Albert, or you could walk to Hyde Park to eat.

2.00 Walk to the traffic lights at the corner of Exhibition and Cromwell Roads. Cross Exhibition Road and go past the Victoria and Albert Museum. Walk to the first bus stop and take a 14 bus.

Get off the bus at Green Park Underground. You will see it on your right. Walk in the same direction as the bus until you come to Albemarle St. Turn left. Cross and walk up Albemarle St and continue walking until you reach the Royal Institution, a building with large pillars. Enter and stop at the desk. The exhibition is down the stairs which are next to the lift.

3.00 **Michael Faraday's Laboratory**

Michael Faraday (1791–1867) was the son of a blacksmith. He had a poor education and was apprenticed to a bookbinder when he was 14. Reading books while binding them stimulated his interest in science, so he began attending lectures at the Royal Institute. He asked Sir Humphrey Davy (1778–1829) to take him on as an assistant in 1813 and in 1833 he succeeded Davy as professor of chemistry.

You can see a lab set out as it would have appeared in Faraday's lifetime. It is arranged for an experiment on diamagnetism (cross-magnetism). In the showroom you can see his medals and personal possessions, a very early Cruickshank battery, the first electric motor, an induction ring, and optical glass made by Faraday.

The nearest underground is Green Park.

Do You Know?
1. What James Watt's rotation beam engine was used for?
2. When Puffing Billy was made?
3. What the forerunner for the Model T Ford was?
4. The name of the man who designed the Rocket engine?
5. What W. H. Fox Talbot invented?
6. What allows you to see above the water when you are in a submarine?
7. The name of a red gemstone?
8. What is ignited on a match to make it burn?
9. What erosion means?
10. What flows from a volcano?

TOUR 12
V for Victory

1 The Cabinet War Rooms, Clive Steps, King
Charles St, London SW1. Tel. (01) 930 6961 or
(01) 735 8922
⊖ Westminster; Bus 3, 11, 12, 24, 29, 53, 70, 77, 77A, 88,
109, 159, 170, 172, 184
10.00–17.50 Tuesday–Sunday; *Closed*: Monday, Good
Friday, 1st Monday May, 24, 25, 26 December, 1 January
A ££, C £, P £, S £; Wheelchair/Shop/Toilet

2 Boats from Westminster to HMS Belfast,
Westminster Passenger Service Association, Westminster
Pier, London W1. Tel. (01) 930 0971
⊖ Westminster
Westminster to Tower: 10.00 and every 20 minutes
A ££, C £
Tower to *HMS Belfast* to *Westminster*
Summer: Daily; Winter: Weekends
A ££, C ££

3 HMS Belfast, Symons Wharf, Vine Lane, Tooley St,
London SE1. Tel. (01) 407 6434 or (01) 735 8922
⊖ London Bridge, Tower Hill; Bus 10, 42, 44, 47, 48, 70,
78
Summer: 11.00–17.50 daily; Winter:11.00–16.30 daily
A ££, C £, P £; Shop/Food/Toilet

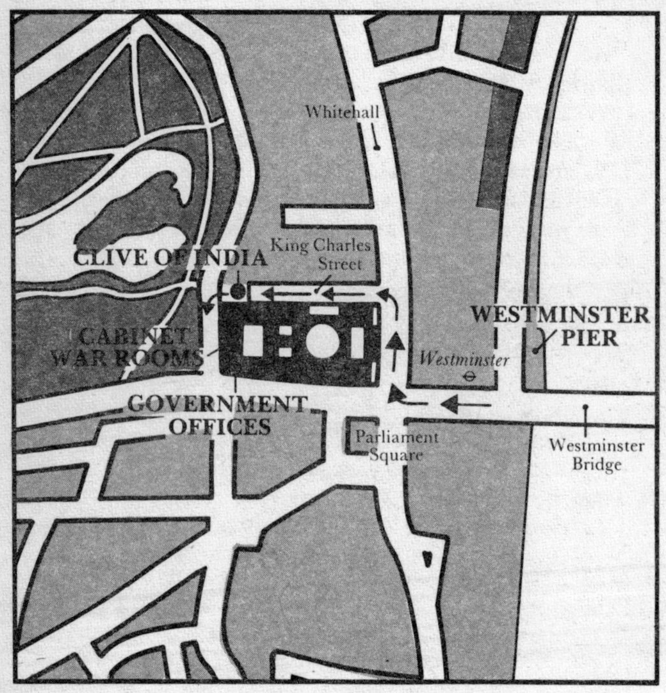

Whitehall
CLIVE OF INDIA
King Charles
Street
WESTMINSTER
PIER
CABINET
WAR ROOMS
Westminster
GOVERNMENT
OFFICES
Parliament
Square
Westminster
Bridge

● Westminster

If possible, it would be best to have a picnic lunch on this tour. St James's Park is beautiful and peaceful, with ducks to feed, wonderful plants and trees, and a view of Buckingham Palace. Or you could eat at one or two places on Bridge Street on the way to Westminster Pier, where you are going to take the boat to HMS *Belfast*.

Go through the barrier and left into the tunnel. As you turn right you will pass the entrance to the Houses of Parliament. When you reach street level, walk straight to the traffic lights, turn right and cross. Then cross Parliament Street and go right. Turn left at King Charles Street. At the end you will see a statue of Clive of India.

Robert, Baron Clive of Passey (1725–74), was a British soldier who joined the East India Company in 1743 and eventually gained complete control of Bengal. Clive was made Governor, but in 1760 he was cited in an enquiry into the Company's affairs. Although acquitted, he committed suicide.

Go down the steps and turn left. You will see the entrance to the Cabinet War Rooms

---

11.00 The Cabinet War Rooms

As early as 1936, the British government felt it important to make plans for protecting the Cabinet and Chiefs of Staff in the case of war with Germany. In 1938, the basement under the western side of the new Public Offices was thought to be suitable, as the building had a steel-frame structure. General Ismay (1887–1965), Chief of Staff to the Minister of Defence, was made responsible for the Central War Room.

The plans gathered impetus during the Munich Crisis and the rooms were equipped with telephones, bedding and food, and the ceilings were reinforced with timber props and steel girders. The need for more rooms grew as the situation worsened; the War Rooms became operational in 1939.

After leaving the first area, which contains information about the War Rooms, you will see the **Cabinet Room**, containing a square hollow table. Churchill sat in the wooden chair facing you. The red and green bulbs indicated whether an air raid was in progress. You will see a seating plan for the table for 15 October 1940. The time is 18.00 and a meeting is about to take place.

As you leave the Cabinet Room, you will pass an opening in the floor. This led to sleeping areas in a sub-basement and was used by shift typists, map readers, or people caught in a raid.

You now pass the door leading to the Cabinet Room. A sentry was stationed here. As you pass the **Officers' Mess and Waiting Room**, notice the raised sill. There is a weather board on the left and the room of Churchill's Principal Private Secretary, one of the four rooms of Churchill's Suite.

Now you will come to a small room on the left, where the transatlantic telephone to Washington was kept, along with a scrambler housing. The Germans were able to unscramble conversations until about 1943, and so a more advanced scrambler was sent to England from the United States of America.

In **Room 60 Left**, you will find a BBC outside broadcasting station, which enabled Churchill to broadcast directly from the War Rooms. **Room 60 Right** was emergency office space for typists.

Room 60A has been restored to look as it did before 1941. It was an office for typists of the Joint Planners. If they were working late, they would go down the hatch in the floor to sleep in the sub-basement.

Room 61 Right was General Ismay's and **Room 61 Left** was an emergency sleeping area for his Private Secretaries.

Room 61A Right was for Sir Edward Bridges, Secretary to the War Cabinet, while **Room 61A Left** was used by his Private Secretaries.

Room 62 was the room of the Advanced Headquarters of the GHQ (General Headquarters) Home Forces. **62A** was for Senior Staff Officers.

Notice the door covered with keys as you go into **62B**. This is where the Camp Commandant had his office.

Room 64 is an overflow map room. There is a large map on the wall and a telephone switch frame.

Room 65 is the main Map Room. Because it is difficult to understand where the people sat, here is a plan of the table.

The coloured phones linked the room to each service War Room. The white telephone near the Duty Officer was connected to 10 Downing Street. The green handsets on several of the phones mean they were fitted with scramblers.

Information was relayed to this room about troop movements, plane missions and battle lines, and the information was plotted on large maps on the walls. One of those maps is still in the Map Room. The men who worked in this room worked in shifts of about six hours.

Room 65A was allocated to Winston Churchill for emergency accommodation, although he only used it three times. He had other rooms on the ground floor of the building which were much more comfortable. He made many of his wartime broadcasts from this room.

Rooms 66 and **66A** were used by the Prime Minister's Staff. **Room 67** was used for different purposes: as part of the map room, an emergency conference room for the Chiefs of Staff and, later in the war, for the Prime Minister's Private Office.

Room 68, where the shop is now, was the Officer's Mess, where they rested in their off-duty hours.

12.00 Boats from Westminster to HMS Belfast
When you leave, go back up the steps to Whitehall, cross the street and continue back to Westminster Bridge. Go down the steps to Westminster Pier and turn left to the ticket office. Buy a one-way ticket to the Tower. Then go down the ramp to the boats. The boats to the Tower leave every 20 minutes.

13.00 When you arrive at Tower Pier, walk to the boat which will ferry you to HMS *Belfast*. Buy a combined ticket for HMS *Belfast* and the return trip to Westminster Pier.

14.00 HMS Belfast
HMS *Belfast* was launched in 1938, but because the ship was badly damaged by a German mine, it needed to be rebuilt and was not seaworthy until 1942. In World War II (1943), it was involved in the Battle of North Cape in which the *Scharnhorst*, a German ship, was sunk, and in 1944 it led the cruiser bombardment supporting the Allied invasion of France. Subsequently HMS *Belfast* provided fire support during the Korean War and, after modernization, it went to the Far East as the flagship of the station. In 1963, its active career ended.

You will start your tour by going to the second ladder on the port side of the boat, which takes you to the **Boat Deck**. You can see the gun emplacements and perhaps sit in the seat of one which has a handle still working so that you can position the gun. A crew of sixteen was needed to operate each of these 4-inch guns.

You can see the anchor on the **Forecastle**.

When you get to the 'A' Turret, you will see three 6-inch guns in it. Each turret needed 27 men, with 22 below in the magazine and shell-room, to operate it. On the left-hand side you can see a photograph of men working a gun like this one.

The **Flag Deck** is where signal messages were sent by using flags or 20-inch projectors; you can see one on each side of the deck.

In the **Director Control Tower**, you will find the master aiming-sight and firing pistol for the 6-inch gun, which was operated electrically.

In good weather, the guns were controlled from the **Gun Direction Platform**. If an enemy was detected, the sight on the centre platform would indicate the target to the 6-inch guns, and the sights on either side to the 4-inch and close-range guns. Also, there were lookouts in the round sights searching the sea and sky for any object.

In the **Operations Room**, as in the Map Room of the Cabinet War Rooms, information was gathered and plotted to help the Captain of the ship make decisions about what action to take. To get this information, men would listen to the radio, use radar, and make soundings on the ocean floor to try to find submarines.

The Captain commanded and controlled the ship, with the help of an Officer of the Watch, from the **Compass Platform**. When they wanted the ship to move in a particular direction, they would talk into a voice-pipe to the Quartermaster, who was below them in a forward position; he would then steer the ship.

The **Bridge Wireless Office** always had an operator in it, regardless of whether the ship was sailing or in port. Whenever a message came in, the operator wrote down that it had come, made copies of it, and gave them to the Captain and other officers.

Because HMS *Belfast* acted as a flagship to the fleet, there is an **Admiral's Bridge**. The Admiral's flag would fly whenever he was on board, and he would stand on this bridge to direct the fleet. The Admiral needed additional communication facilities, accommodation for his staff and himself, and extra operational equipment.

There is a **Damage Control Display** which shows how a gap in the wall was repaired, and an injured person receiving help.

The **6-inch Transmitting Station** has a fire-control table to help solve the complicated calculations needed to hit a target a long way away while it and HMS *Belfast* were moving.

You will see the living accommodation necessary to sustain about 800 people for months at a time. Not only did the bakers bake bread for the staff of HMS *Belfast*, they also made bread to make up the rations for the other ships of the fleet.

You will see the **Messdeck of 1939** and be able to compare it with a modern messdeck; you can also see the **Sick Bay, the Dental Surgery**, the **Galley**, where the meals were prepared, the **Bakery**, the **Chapel**, the **Laundry**, and the rooms of the Admiral, Captain, Officers and ratings.

Did You Spot?

1. What is keeping the *Belfast* secure?

Do You Know?

2. The year war was declared on Germany?
3. The name given to the time in 1940 when there was heavy bombing of England?
4. Why is there a raised sill outside the Officer's Mess?
5. What BBC stands for?
6. What the Camp Commandant's job dealt with?
7. What HMS stands for?
8. Who launched HMS *Belfast*?
9. What kind of mine damaged the *Belfast*?
10. What the Allied Invasion was called?

TOUR 13
Elegant London

1 Harrods, Knightsbridge, London SW1.
Tel. (01) 730 1234
⊖ Knightsbridge; Bus 9, 19, 22, 52, 73, 137
09.00–18.00 Monday, Tuesday, Thursday, Friday
09.00–19.00 Wednesday
09.00–17.00 Saturday
Wheelchair/Toilet/Food

2 Burlington Arcade, Piccadilly, London W1.
⊖ Piccadilly Circus
Closed: Sunday

3 Sotheby's, 34 New Bond St, London W1.
Tel. (01) 493 8080
⊖ Bond Street, Oxford Circus
Closed: Saturday and Sunday

4 South Molton Street, London W1.
⊖ Bond Street, Oxford Circus

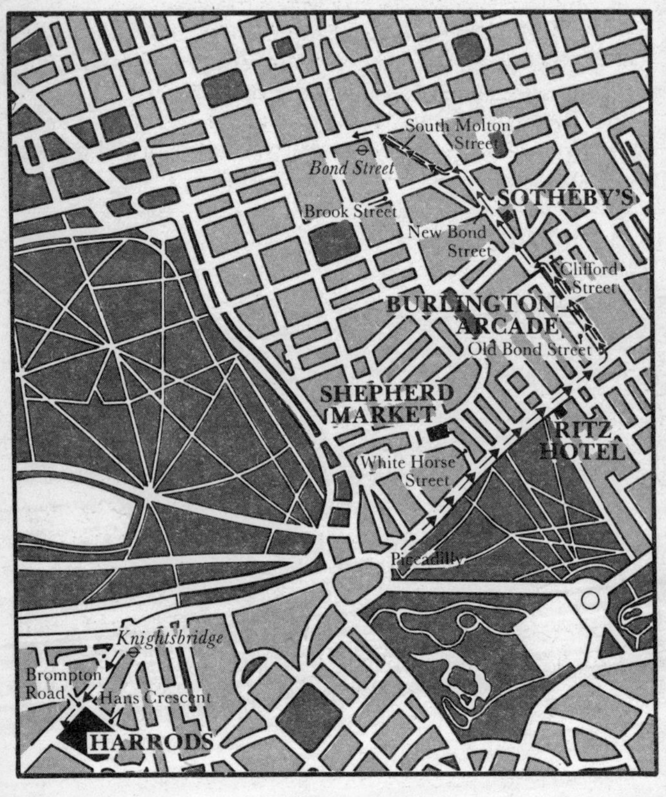

South Molton Street
Bond Street
Brook Street
SOTHEBY'S
New Bond Street
Clifford Street
BURLINGTON ARCADE
Old Bond Street
SHEPHERD MARKET
RITZ HOTEL
White Horse Street
Piccadilly
Knightsbridge
Brompton Road
Hans Crescent
HARRODS

⊖ Knightsbridge

When you leave Knightsbridge Underground, you will see Harrods directly across the street.

Walk to the front of the building and go in at Door No. 7. There are doormen in green coats which match the colour of the awnings over the window.

It would be helpful to get a guide to the store as it is very large, with several lifts, escalators and flights of stairs.

10.00 Harrods

Harrods first opened in 1849 in premises at 105 Brompton Road. The store gradually acquired more property, grew larger and, in 1901, the store you see today was built. The site Harrods stands on covers 4½ acres, and if you add all the floors together, the selling space would cover 15½ acres; it has 72 window displays.

Among other things, Harrods will organize your funeral, reblock your hats, fill your deep freeze, lend you books, tune your piano, test your eyes, massage your feet, and trace your family history.

They have had record-breaking sales of 120 tons of Christmas Puddings, 30,000 Hot Cross Buns, 130 different types of bread, and have displayed a Sturgeon fish weighing over 500 lb which was 11 feet 6 inches long.

Go right once inside Door No. 7 and walk until you get halfway through Haberdashery. Turn left into the **Food Halls**.

Here you will see the most fantastic selection of foods of all kinds, housed in what is called 'art nouveau' decoration – a style of tiled walls and ceilings. These Halls were built between 1901 and 1905. You will find bread, cakes, a delicatessen, confectionery, vegetables, wine and many other delicious delicacies. The Meat Hall is the most interesting, the tiles being made by the firm of Royal Doulton.

Take the lift near Perfumery and Cosmetics and go to the First Floor.

On this floor are **Junior Fashions** and the **Children's Shop** near the lifts. There is a children's hairdresser, clothing for girls and boys from 2 to 7, fashions for girls aged 8–16, and a **Baby Shop**.

Take the lift up to the Second Floor. The **Pet Shop** is above the Baby Shop and has everything your pet has ever wanted – collars, food, leads, houses, beds, toys, and coats. You can also buy your pets here – pedigree dogs, fish, guinea pigs and hamsters, pedigree kittens, and large birds that have been hand-reared and trained for Harrods.

Now take the same lift to the Fourth Floor. When you get out, go the opposite way from the direction you took on the other floors. Walk through the area where theatre bookings are made, through the first part of Travel Goods, into the second Travel Goods, and then turn left. You will come to the **Boys' Section**.

Go through the Musical Instruments to the **Toys**. Some of the more splendid toys are tractors, telescopes, a Range Rover, caravan and huge teddy bears and rocking horses.

Go down the escalators by the Toy Department until you reach the ground floor. Then go through Pharmacy, Handbags and Stationery, and out through Door 8 to Brompton Road.

12.00   Three suggestions for lunch:

1. You can eat at Harrods which, as you might have guessed, is rather expensive.

2. Have lunch at the Ritz, which is even more expensive than Harrods, but is quite an experience. To get

to the Ritz, take the bus to Green Park, get off at the stop near Green Park Underground, and cross Piccadilly to the Ritz.

3. You can eat at a nearby pub or restaurant if Harrods or the Ritz is not your style. Take the bus to Green Park, and get off just after the pedestrian traffic lights; then walk to White Horse Lane, turn left and walk to Shepherd Market, where there are a number of restaurants and pubs with outside seating.

Cross Brompton Road and go to the bus stop. Take a No. 14 bus to Piccadilly. It is best to check with the conductor if the bus is going to Piccadilly because in heavy traffic they only go as far as Green Park. The conductor will tell you which bus to take.

After you have eaten, walk up Piccadilly on the left side until you get to the Burlington Arcade. Turn left into it.

13.30 Burlington Arcade

The Burlington Arcade was built in 1819 and contains shops selling expensive, high-quality clothes, jewellery and antiques. You will see a watchman, called a Beadle, at one end. He closes the gates at night and opens them again in the morning.

Sotheby's

Cross and turn into Cork Street, where you will see several art galleries. Cross Clifford Street, go left and then right into New Bond Street.

You will pass shops selling old paintings, silver items, fashionable clothes and eventually you will come to **Sotheby's**, the world-famous auction house, on the right. There are auctions Monday to Thursday and on Friday you can view items to be auctioned.

South Molton Street

If you have been to Sotheby's, cross to the other side
of New Bond Street, turn left on Brook Street and
then right on South Molton Street.

South Molton Street is now a pedestrian walkway
with pavement cafés and shops selling some of London's most exclusive clothes accessories.

At the top of South Molton Street is Bond Street
Underground.

TOUR 14
Stars and Waxworks

1 Madame Tussaud's, Marylebone Rd, London NW1.
Tel. (01) 935 6861
⊖ Baker Street; Bus 18, 27, 30, 176 pass door, 2, 13, 74,
113, 159 nearby
Summer: 09.30–17.30 daily; Winter: 10.00–17.30 daily
Closed: Christmas Day
A £££, C ££, P ££; Wheelchair/Shop/Food/Toilet

2 The London Planetarium, Marylebone Rd,
London NW1. Tel. (01) 486 1121
⊖ Baker Street; Bus 18, 27, 30, 176 pass door, 2, 13, 74,
113, 159 nearby
11.00–16.30 daily. *Closed*: Christmas Day
A ££, C ££, P ££
*Combined tickets for Madame Tussaud's and The London
Planetarium*
A £££, C ££, P £££

3 Regent's Park, London NW1.
⊖ Baker Street, Camden Town

REGENT'S
PARK
Allsop Place
Marylebone Road
MADAME TUSSAUD'S
Baker Street
LONDON
PLANETARIUM
Baker Street

⊖ Baker Street

Because Madame Tussaud's has long queues in the summer, try to arrive as early as possible. If not, you will have to queue for up to 45 minutes. If you cannot arrive early in the morning, the next best time is about 14.00.

Baker Street is where Sherlock Holmes lived in the 1800s, but it has changed since Sir Arthur Conan Doyle wrote his stories of mystery and intrigue.

When you arrive at Baker Street, pass the Marylebone exit and go to the right after the ticket barrier. While in the underground station you will pass a café where you can buy sandwiches for a picnic lunch later. Turn left once you arrive in the street.

09.30 Madame Tussaud's

Mme Tussaud was born in 1761 in Strasbourg. She learned wax modelling from a Dr Curtius, and during the French Revolution was ordered to make wax death-masks of the guillotine victims. When Dr Curtius died, she inherited his wax exhibition.

Mme Tussaud emigrated to England from France in 1802. She mainly toured around the country with her exhibition until 1835, when she finally settled down in Portland Square at the age of 74. She must have been a very spirited woman to work to such an age, and to do the work she did during the revolution in France. Mme Tussaud died when she was 89 years old, and if you look carefully, you will see a wax figure which she made of herself when she was 81.

You will also see many other French figures made by Mme Tussaud, such as Voltaire (1694–1778), the writer, Marie Antoinette (1755–93) and Louis XVI (1754–93) with their two children, and also their severed heads, made from death-masks, in the Chamber of Horrors next to the actual guillotine blade.

Madame Tussaud, after the painting
by Paul Fischer, 1845

Start the exhibition in the **Conservatory** where you will find figures of many popular people you will be familiar with – the Beatles, Agatha Christie, Severiano Ballesteros and many more. You will then see the **Superstars** – Dolly Parton, Michael Jackson, Boy George and David Bowie, each singing a song.

The **Grand Hall** has historical figures, most of whom are English, but also foreign Presidents or other important people. One of the better groups is that of Henry VIII and his six wives. You can stand next to Napoleon, Queen Elizabeth I, or Charles Dickens.

The **Chamber of Horrors** is not for the squeamish. You will find once-popular methods of ridding society of its undesirables and will see settings of murders and the murderers. You will walk down a dank, murky street from Jack the Ripper's London and see his last victim unaware that she is about to die.

Now you can visit a reconstruction of the **Battle of Trafalgar** with all the sounds of cannons firing and ships creaking and colliding. You can see the living conditions of the sailors on ships like HMS *Victory* and see Nelson as he lay dying.

11.00 The London Planetarium

Go into the **Astronomer's Gallery** where you will see:

Claudio Ptolemy (pronounced Tol-eh-me) who lived in the 2nd Century in Alexandria, Egypt. He was a famous mathematician, astronomer and geographer and wrote many books. Ptolemy believed that the planets moved round the earth.

Nicolaus Copernicus, born in 1473 in Poland, was the first person to think that the earth moved round the sun. Because the religious thought of the day believed that the earth was at the centre of the universe, he was careful to tell only a few of his friends of his theory.

Galileo Galilei, born in Pisa, Italy in 1564, learned about the invention of the telescope and had one designed for himself. He discovered sunspots and Jupiter's satellites. In 1632 he wrote a book criticizing Ptolemy's ideas and praising Copernicus. This was unwise of him, because in 1616 the Roman Catholic Church had condemned Copernicus. Galileo was sent before an Inquisition Judge and was given the choice of retracting what he had written or death. He retracted, but was placed under house arrest until he died in 1642.

Isaac Newton was born in Lincolnshire in 1642 and went to Cambridge University where he became a professor at the age of 27. Newton is considered to be one of the greatest scientists of all time, discovering the law of gravity and inventing a method of analysis called calculus.

Albert Einstein, born in 1879 in Germany, first developed his theory of relativity while he was working in Switzerland in the early 1900s. In 1921, he received the Nobel Prize for Physics. When World War II began, he went to the United States and remained there until he died in 1955. His theories made it possible to build the atomic bomb which destroyed the Japanese cities of Hiroshima and Nagasaki at the end of World War II.

Now walk up a ramp to the Planetarium where you will see the sky in beautiful detail – the planets, comets and galaxies.

12.00 When you leave the Planetarium go down Allsop Place (along the side of Madame Tussaud's) to the Clarence Gate of Regent's Park. Cross over to the park entrance and go through the laid-out flower beds until you come to the lake. Here you will find seats to rest on, ducks to feed, and hopefully a band playing in the bandstand across the lake – a beautiful place to eat a packed lunch.

12.15 Regent's Park

Regent's Park began as part of Henry VIII's hunting area, which stretched from Kensington Park to Hampstead in the north. John Nash (1752–1835) designed the park and the terraced houses round it. It was opened to the public in 1838 and has been in constant use ever since.

You may see archers practising Robin Hood's old art, listen to the summer Sunday concerts by the lake, or you can rent a boat for a gentle ride among the ducks. There is a beautiful Queen Mary's Garden, with its sculpted hedges and lovely roses; and on Easter Monday morning there is the London Harness Horse Parade, where hundreds of horses parade past, from dray-horses pulling brewery wagons to little ponies and carts.

Did You Spot?

1. The person standing with Napoleon?
2. What sailors slept in on board HMS *Victory*?

Do You Know?

3. Who supposedly ordered the deaths of the little princes in the Tower?
4. What hand-sign Winston Churchill used during World War II?
5. Who the people were questioning the little boy?
6. The name of the story Hans Christian Andersen wrote about a duck?
7. What was hiding in the skirts of Mary Queen of Scots as she was waiting to be executed?
8. Who the model was for the Sleeping Beauty?
9. What country Abraham Lincoln was President of?
10. King Richard I's nickname?

TOUR 15
Dick Turpin and Highwaymen: Attacks on Hampstead Heath

1 Hampstead Heath, Heath Road, London NW3.
⊖ Hampstead; Archway or Golders Green then Bus 210
Bus Green Line 734

2 Kenwood House, Hampstead Lane, London NW3.
Tel. (01) 348 1286/7
⊖ Hampstead; Archway or Golders Green then Bus 210
Bus Green Line 734
April–September: 10.00–19.00 daily
February, March and October: 10.00–17.00 daily
November–January: 10.00–16.00 daily
Closed: Good Friday, 24, 25 December
Wheelchair/Shop/Toilet

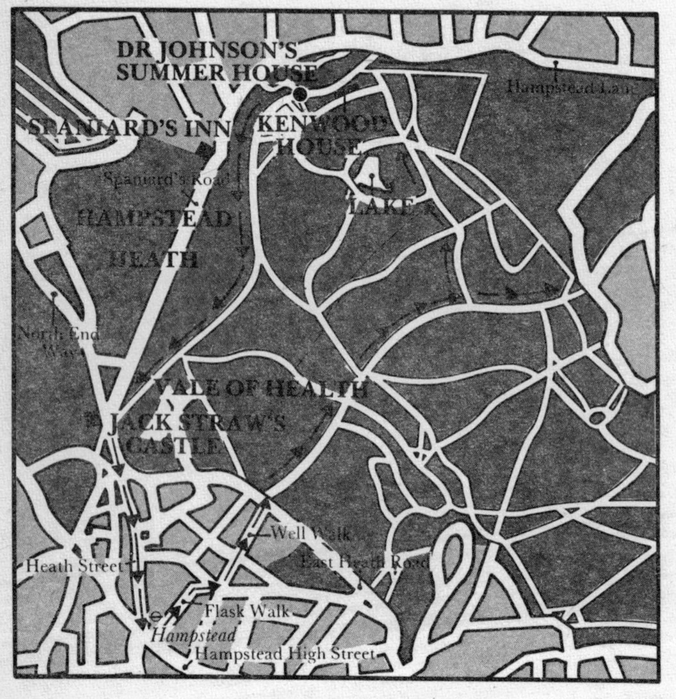

DR JOHNSON'S
SUMMER HOUSE
Hampstead Lane
SPANIARD'S INN
KENWOOD HOUSE
Spaniard's Road
HAMPSTEAD
HEATH
LAKE
North End Way
VALE OF HEALTH
JACK STRAW'S CASTLE
Well Walk
Heath Street
East Heath Road
Flask Walk
Hampstead
Hampstead High Street

⊖ Hampstead

As you pass Parliament Hill, keep an eye on the weather forecast. If it is a windy day take a kite, as Parliament Hill is an excellent kite-flying location.

10.30 Hampstead

Hampstead grew from a small village outside London into a fashionable residential area in the 1800s, when most of the houses were built.

Leave Hampstead Underground to the left and then go left again at the traffic lights. Walk down Hampstead High Street and turn left into Flask Walk.

You will pass several bookshops and the Flask Pub, which serves good food and good draught beer. Stay to the right so that you meet up with the road which is to your right. After crossing New End Square, you will be in Well Walk. Carry on. Walk past the Wells Tavern. On your right is a blue plaque saying John Constable (1776–1837) lived there.

Cross East Heath Road and you are on Hampstead Heath.

11.00 Hampstead Heath

Hampstead Heath covers more than 800 acres and at one time was included in the hunting forest of Henry VIII which stretched to St James's Park.

The Heath plays a great part in the lives of North Londoners with its beautiful untamed scenery, fairs, concerts, swimming and fishing.

Go straight along the broad path. You will mingle with joggers, meet dogs and their owners taking strolls, and hear the sound of birds' singing. You will pass a grassy area and a little way on to the right will be Parliament Hill, where you can fly your kite (if you brought one).

As you walk through the trees, think what it was

like in the 1700s when bandits stopped people as they went home and robbed them of their money and, at times, their lives.

You will approach two ponds: the Boating Pond is on the right and a bird sanctuary on the left. There are toilets at the top of this path. This is a good place to sit down and have a rest.

When you are ready to leave, retrace your steps and move to the right down the slope. Continue walking and go straight through the gates that surround Kenwood. Continue straight on.

You will see a lake on your left. During the summer classical concerts are held here on Saturday nights.

Walk up the hill to Kenwood House. As you approach it, you will see the Coach House. There is a cafeteria, toilets and a restaurant, which is not always open.

Go back up the steps to the path and walk along the side of Kenwood House. Just as the house ends, you will see an ivy pergola. Go through it and walk to the back of the house where you will find the entrance.

11.45 Kenwood House

The first house on this site was built about 1616. It had a succession of owners and in 1754 it was sold to William Murray, the first Earl of Mansfield. Ten years after buying it, he asked Robert Adam (1728–92) to remodel the house. The house remained in the hands of the Murray family until 1912. The last Earl wanted to sell the entire Kenwood estate, about 200 acres, to a building syndicate. However, an appeal was launched to raise funds to buy it publicly and the purchase was finally completed when Edward Cecil Guinness (1847–1927), first Earl of Iveagh, purchased Kenwood and some land from the Earl of Mansfield. He then bequeathed his purchase to the Trustees for the public, furnished the house and installed the collection of paintings.

From the Entrance Hall, go through the top left-hand door and into a passageway. There are interesting chairs with lions and dogs carved on them and a gold clock made for George III (1738–1820) in 1772.

Go into the room near the clock (**Marble Room**) and then into the room on the left. This is the **Dining Room** and was built in 1760. Sitting on the fireplace are black ewers (water jugs) made by Wedgwood. There is a Peter Paul Rubens (1577–1640) painting hanging over the fireplace. There is also a painting of James Stewart, Duke of Richmond, and Rembrandt's (1606–99) 'Self-Portrait'.

Now go out, cross through the Marble Room into the room opposite (**Vestibule**) and into the room on the left.

The **Library** is considered to be the supreme example of an Adams interior. It has a moulded dome ceiling of pink, blue, white and gold. There are shutters on the windows and the books are at the curved ends of the room. Notice the library steps.

Go out and across to **Lord Mansfield's Dressing Room**. Since the bedrooms were on the floor above, it is thought that this was a private room for relaxing. There are paintings by Sir Joshua Reynolds (1723–92) and Thomas Gainsborough (1727–88).

The next room to visit is the **Parlour**. Over the fireplace is a painting of William Pitt (1759–1806), a Prime Minister, by Gainsborough. There is also an interesting painting of Old London Bridge in 1630. Notice how some houses have rooms hanging over the edge of the bridge. Do you see the pub sign cn the right? There are barges on the river and one barge looks like a smaller version of Queen Mary's (1662–94) shallop (in the National Maritime Museum at Greenwich).

Now go into **Lady Mansfield's Dressing Room**. Over the fireplace, there is a miniature of Robert Adam and his designs for mirrors and furniture for the house. There are bills from the Adam Brothers for work finished and an agreement between Lord Mansfield, Thomas Chippendale and Robert Adam.

In the **Housekeeper's Room** are paintings by the Italian artist Pannini.

You now go into the **Orangery**, where there are several paintings, one of two dogs having a fight. In the **Lobby** is a painting of Lady Emma Hamilton (1761–1815). The **Music Room** has a spinet, harp and music stand as well as paintings.

You exit through the shop. Go on the centre-left path. You will go through another ivy pergola. The steps to the right lead to Dr Johnson's summer house. Samuel Johnson (1709–84) was a poet, philosopher and critic and wrote a dictionary which was in print for 100 years.

13.30 When you leave Dr Johnson's summer house carry on until you come to a fork in the road. Go left and then right out of the Kenwood Gates.

Veer right and continue walking. You will begin to go up round the Vale of Health, which is to your left. John Keats the poet (1795–1821) lived here, as did the famous authors D. H. Lawrence (1885–1930) and Edgar Wallace (1875–1932). You are walking in the area where large fairs are held every year.

Just north is the Spaniard's Inn, a well-known pub frequented by Dick Turpin (1706–39). There is a rumour that Turpin was friendly with the landlord of the pub, who gave him keys to the toll gate across the road next to the pub and to a secret door connecting the inn with the stables, thus allowing him to make his escape.

When you get to Spaniards Road, go left. On your right, you will see Jack Straw's Castle, which sits on the highest part of Hampstead Heath. This pub, first recorded in 1713, was destroyed by a bomb during the

War and was rebuilt in 1962. Dickens enjoyed walking over the Heath to have a dinner of meat of wine at Jack Straw's.

Carry on walking down Heath Street, passing the shops and restaurants, until you reach the traffic lights. The entrance to the Underground is around the corner.

Did You Spot?

1. Another animal painting by Gainsborough. What was it about?

Do You Know?

2. What John Constable is famous for?
3. Where kites originated?
4. What fruit grows on oak trees?
5. Where the Stuart line of Kings came from?
6. What war was fought when George III was King?
7. What Chippendale was famous for?
8. Where Dick Turpin was hanged?
9. The name of the book by Charles Dickens which has the word 'papers' in it?

TOUR 16
Masks and Magic

1 The Museum of Mankind, 6 Burlington Gardens, London W1. Tel. (01) 437 2224
⊖ Green Park, Piccadilly Circus; Bus 3, 6, 9, 9A, 12, 13, 14, 15, 19, 19A, 22, 25, 38, 39, 53, 55, 59, 88, 159
10.00–17.00 Monday–Saturday; 14.30–18.00 Sunday.
Closed: Good Friday, 1st Monday in May, 24, 25, 26 December, 1 January
Wheelchair (no toilet)/Shop/Toilet

2 Burlington Arcade, Piccadilly, London W1.
⊖ Piccadilly Circus
Closed: Sunday

3 Fortnum and Mason, Piccadilly, London W1.
⊖ Piccadilly Circus
Closed: Sunday

4 London Brass Rubbing Centre, St James's Church, Piccadilly, London W1. Tel. (01) 437 6023
⊖ Piccadilly Circus; Bus 3, 6, 9, 9A, 12 ,13, 14, 15, 19, 19A, 22, 25, 38, 39, 53, 55, 59, 88, 159
10.00–18.00 Monday–Saturday; 12.00–18.00 Sunday
Closed: 25 December
Shop/Toilet/Food

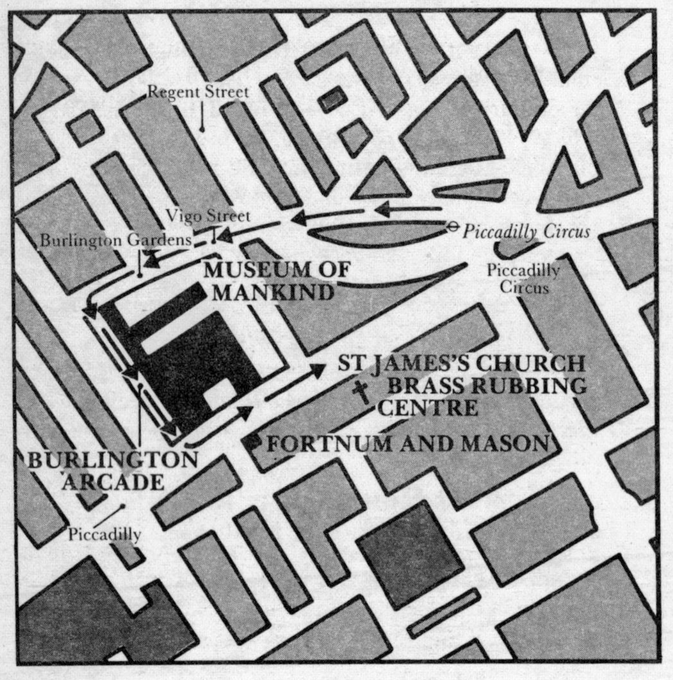

Regent Street
Vigo Street
Burlington Gardens
MUSEUM OF
MANKIND
Piccadilly Circus
Piccadilly
Circus
ST JAMES'S CHURCH
BRASS RUBBING
CENTRE
FORTNUM AND MASON
BURLINGTON
ARCADE
Piccadilly

⊖ Piccadilly Circus

Try to time your tour to arrive at the traffic lights opposite Fortnum and Mason so that you can see the clock chime on the hour.

After you pass through the barrier, leave the underground by way of Subway 2. The Museum of Mankind is indicated. Go up the stairs to Regent Street. As you get to street level, you will see behind you Lilywhites, which has a comprehensive Sports Department.

Walk up Regent Street, passing what is called 'The Quadrant', built between 1817 and 1825 and designed by John Nash (1752–1835). Go left into Vigo Street, which runs into Burlington Gardens. The Museum of Mankind will be on your left.

10.30 The Museum of Mankind

This Museum has continually changing exhibitions to allow it to put on show all of the items in its possession. There is one main exhibition which lasts about two years.

The current one is on the Amazonian Indians. You can see clothing, boats, poison spears and darts, pottery, jewellery, musical instruments, shrunken heads, ceremonial costumes, etc. Walk into a typical Maloca (house) of the Tukano tribe and see how a family used the items you have just seen on exhibit.

Walk through Burlington Arcade

Turn left when you leave the Museum. Go left, immediately after passing Cork Street, into Burlington Arcade.

Burlington Arcade was built in 1819 and contains very expensive shops selling clothes, jewellery and antiques. There are watchmen who close the doors when the day is finished.

At the end of Burlington Arcade is Piccadilly. Walk

to the left past the Royal Academy of Arts. Before you cross at the traffic lights, look at the clock on the outside of Fortnum and Mason.

11.00 Look inside Fortnum and Mason

Fortnum and Mason is a famous London shop selling, on the ground floor, food and wine. Go in and have a quick look around. Inside, you will see chandeliers, two old statues of servants with platters and thousands of tasty delicacies.

Carry on walking down Piccadilly until you come to St James's Church. Go into the church and have a look at the Wren interior. Then go out and turn left through the bookshop. Turn left when you reach the street until you come to some steps on the left leading to the Brass Rubbing Centre.

12.30 The London Brass Rubbing Centre

The Centre has a large number of brass plates from tombs which make very good pictures to hang on a wall as a souvenir.

You can do rubbings of the brasses of:

William Shakespeare (1564–1616), who was born and died at Stratford-upon-Avon, but worked for most of his life in London. The first collected edition of his works, known as the First Folio, was printed in 1623.

Sir John (d. 1380) and Lady de la Pole. Sir John was a knight in the service of John of Gaunt (1340–99), the Duke of Lancaster, who was the son of Edward III (1312–77).

St Thomas à Becket (1118–70), the Archbishop of Canterbury during the reign of Henry II (1133–89). He was murdered by supporters of the King as he fought Henry over his conviction that criminal clergy should stand trial in a church court, not in a royal court.

Robert the Bruce (1274–1329), King of the Scots.

He was forced into exile by Edward I but defeated the English army at Bannockburn in 1314.

Thomas Chaucer, son of the author Geoffrey Chaucer (1340–1400). He was also a retainer of John of Gaunt and was speaker of the House of Commons several times. His mother was the sister of John of Gaunt's third wife.

Your closest Underground Station is Piccadilly Circus.

Did You Spot?
1. What happened when the clock chimed the hour?
2. What the men who work in Fortnum and Mason are wearing?

Do You Know?
3. Wren's Christian name?
4. Who Anne Boleyn was married to?
5. A well-known story about Robert the Bruce? What insect did it involve?

TOUR 17
Paintings, Hamley's, and Liberty's

1 The National Gallery, Trafalgar Square, London
WC2. Tel. (01) 839 3321; recorded information
(01) 839 3526
⊖ Charing Cross, Leicester Square; Bus 1, 3, 6, 9, 11, 12,
13, 15, 23, 24, 29, 53, 77, 77A, 88, 159, 168, 170, 172, 176
10.00–18.00 Monday–Saturday; 14.00–18.00 Sunday
Closed: Good Friday, 1st Monday May, 24, 25 December,
1 January
Wheelchair/Shop/Food/Toilet

2 Trafalgar Square, London WC2
⊖ Charing Cross, Leicester Square; Bus 1, 3, 6, 9, 11, 12,
13, 15, 23, 24, 29, 53, 77, 77A, 88, 159, 168, 170, 172, 176

3 Hamley's Toy Shop, 188–96 Regent St,
London W1. Tel. (01) 734 3161
⊖ Oxford Circus, Piccadilly Circus; Bus 3, 6, 12, 15, 23,
53, 88, 159
09.00–17.30 Monday–Saturday
Closed: Sunday, Good Friday, 24, 25, 26 December,
1 January
Wheelchair/Food/Toilet

4 Liberty's, Regent St, London W1. Tel. (01) 734 1234
⊖ Oxford Circus
09.00–17.30 Monday–Saturday
Closed: Sunday, Good Friday, 24, 25, 26 December,
1 January

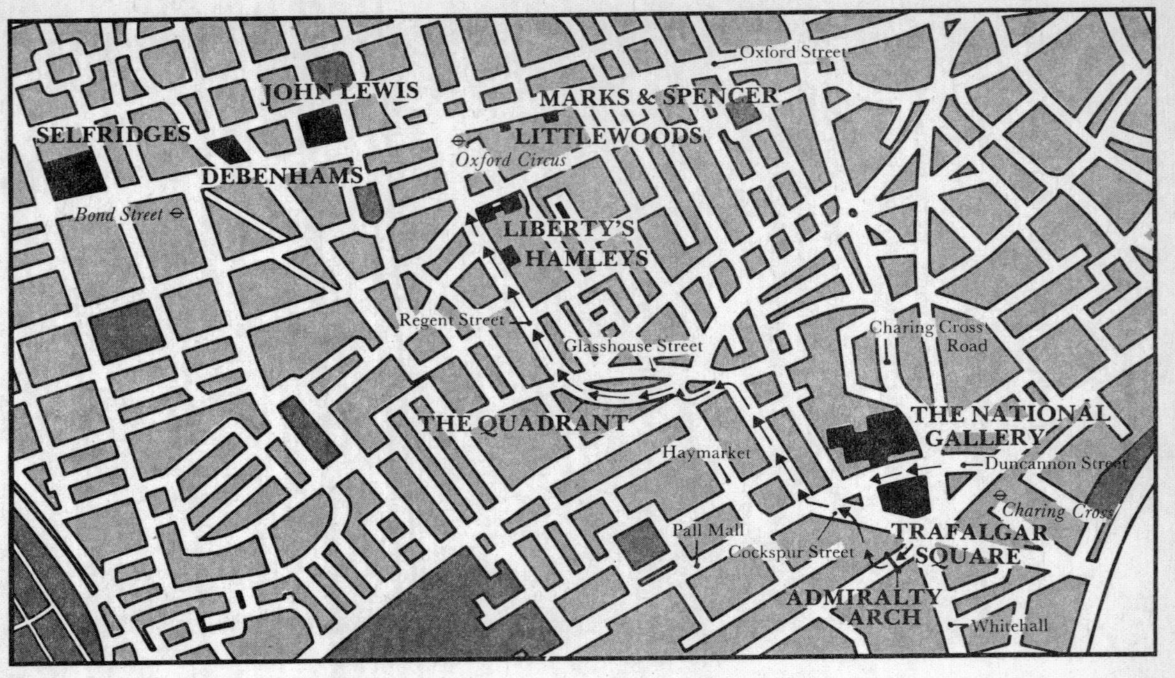

Oxford Street
SELFRIDGES
JOHN LEWIS
MARKS & SPENCER
LITTLEWOODS
Oxford Circus
DEBENHAMS
Bond Street
LIBERTY'S
HAMLEYS
Regent Street
Glasshouse Street
Charing Cross Road
THE QUADRANT
THE NATIONAL GALLERY
Duncannon Street
Charing Cross
Haymarket
Pall Mall
Cockspur Street
TRAFALGAR SQUARE
ADMIRALTY ARCH
Whitehall

⊖ Charing Cross

At Charing Cross Underground, go to the right after passing through the barrier and out of the exit for Trafalgar Square. Veer right at the junction and go up the stairs.

Go straight down Duncannon Street, cross to the Church of St Martin in the Fields, and then cross left at St Martin's Place. Walk straight ahead. Look at Nelson's Column. Although his back is towards you, it is still quite imposing and there is a very good view of Westminster and Big Ben behind the column.

10.30 The National Gallery

Go up the first steps in the Gallery, turn left and go up more steps into **Room 1**.

Through the doors, you will see a small room ahead of you and a small hinged painting of Richard II (1363–1400) kneeling to the Virgin Mary; this was painted in about 1395.

In **Room 2**, there is a painting by Paolo Uccello (c. 1397–1475) of a battle. Notice the very long lances being carried by the knights.

Walk through **Rooms 4** and **6** and turn into **Room 7** where you will find a grey chalk drawing by Leonardo da Vinci (1452–1519), probably a sketch for a painting. As well as being a famous painter ('Mona Lisa'), he was interested in anatomy, botany, geology, hydraulics and mechanics.

Go out of **Room 7** into **Rooms 8** and **9**. Look at the carved chests from the middle 1500s. Turn right in the middle of the room and go into **Room 10**.

Here are five portraits painted between 1400 and 1500. The centre one is of the Doge Leonardo Loredan by Giovanni Bellini (c. 1459–1516). Notice how the blue of the background makes the costume outline very clear.

Walk back to Room 9 and turn into **Room 15**. Find the painting of the boy and girl by Judith Leyster, and then go into **Room 17** and look at the 'Still Life' of Jan van Huysum (1682–1749).

Go into **Room 18** and pass through **Room 19** into **Room 25**. The large painting of two men is by Hans Holbein the younger (1497–1543), who lived in London during the reign of Henry VIII (1491–1547) and was the court painter. Jean de Dinteville, the man on the left, asked Holbein to paint it showing the interests of the two men. On the dagger in Dinteville's hand is his age – 29. The age of the other man, George de Selve, is 25, and is written on the book.

Behind you is a portrait of Christine of Denmark, which Holbein painted for Henry VIII to look at because he was interested in marrying her. He also painted a portrait of Anne of Cleves (1515–57), one of Henry's wives. It is said that Holbein improved her looks in the painting and when Henry finally saw her, he was very unhappy and divorced her quite soon after the marriage.

Go into **Room 24**. At the end of the room is the painting called 'The Marriage' by Jan van Eyck (d. 1441). It was painted in 1434 to commemorate the marriage of Giovanni Arnolfini and his wife, Giovanna Cenami.

Go back to Room 25 and then go left and left again to **Room 26**. Here is a self-portrait of Rembrandt (1606–69) when he was about 30. Rembrandt was a very successful teacher, painter and collector of many works of art. He went bankrupt and spent the last 20 years of his life in isolation, during which time he painted some of his best work. Go into **Room 27** and you will see a very different self-portrait painted when he was 60.

Go out to the room with the lights and then right. This is **Room 28**. On the right side are small paintings of girls playing an instrument by Jan Veermer

(1632–75). Look at the water pump in the painting by Pieter de Hooch.

Now go back to the left and through **Room 29**. Turn right in the middle and you will be in the Shop.

Walk out and cross Trafalgar Square at the lights.

12.00 Trafalgar Square

You can sit and eat your lunch or rest your feet. You will see pigeons sitting on people's hands, feet, heads or arms while eating seed (which you can buy if you want to feed them). Climb the lions, but be careful coming down.

Trafalgar Square is named after the battle Horatio Nelson (1758–1805) fought and won against the French; he was killed during the fighting.

The statue of Charles I (1600–1649) stands facing Banqueting House, from which he walked to his execution. It was made in 1633 while he was still alive.

13.00 Leave Trafalgar Square by crossing at the traffic lights at the south-east corner of the Square. Go down the subway, walking through the underground station, to the other end of the tunnel and up the stairs.

Turn left at the top and you will see Admiralty Arch. This was built as a tribute to Queen Victoria (1819–1901).

The next part of the tour takes you up Haymarket and Regent Street to Hamley's. If you do not want to walk this far you can either take the underground to Piccadilly and pick the tour up there, or you can walk down Whitehall to a bus stop for buses 3, 12 or 88, all going up Regent Street.

Walk through the Arch and in the distance you will see Queen Victoria's Monument and Buckingham Palace. Turn right into Spring Gardens and then go left.

When you get to the traffic lights by Barclays Bank, cross to the centre of the street and then go left. Walk up Haymarket.

On your right, you will pass the Theatre Royal, which was designed by John Nash (1752–1835). Charles Dickens (1812–70) had a reserved box here and put on productions in which he acted with a group of actor friends.

If you didn't eat at Trafalgar Square, you will pass several places to eat. At the top of Haymarket is Piccadilly Circus. Go left and cross the southern part of Regent Street and then Piccadilly. Go straight on then left onto Regent Street.

The buildings along both sides of the street – called 'The Quadrant' – were built between 1817 and 1825 and designed by John Nash who, at the same time, designed Regent's Park.

Cross to the opposite side of Regent Street. Continue walking, going past Gerrard the jewellers, Carnaby Street, the famous ceramic firm of Wedgwood, and Mappin and Webb – Hamley's is just to your right.

13.30 Hamley's Toy Shop

William Hamley started his first toy shop, called 'Noah's Ark', in 1760. Because of the selection and quality of his toys, his business went from strength to strength and they moved to Regent Street from High Holborn in 1881. Hamley's also bought 'Blands', a famous conjuring and magic business. They imported dolls and sold chemistry and scientific sets and model steam engines. They were the first to sell a new game called 'Cossima', which was later renamed 'ping-pong'.

Here is a list of the wonderful toys you will find on each floor:

Lower Ground:
Mechanical toys, party equipment, magic and jokes, rocking horses

Ground:
Stuffed toys, puppets, Lego

First:
Model soldiers, paints, trains, scenery, models to build, kites

Second:
Rag, porcelain, Barbie dolls, doll's houses and furniture, young children's toys and clothes

Third:
Sportswear and sports equipment, computer games

Fourth:
Puzzles, books, restaurant

Leave Hamley's to the right. Continue walking up Regent Street until you come to Liberty's, one of London's most famous department stores. If you are not too tired, walk in and look at the mock Tudor part of the building.

14.00 Liberty's

Liberty's was founded in 1875 by Arthur Liberty. At first he imported oriental materials, but he grew dissatisfied because his suppliers began to change the subtle colouring to colours they thought Europeans would like. In 1882, he began experimenting with dying Indian cashmere and silk – soft, light materials which hung very differently and gave women more freedom of movement than the clothes which were very fashionable at the time. Liberty's style was taken up by the Aesthetic Movement, the arch aesthete being Oscar Wilde. Their slogan was 'art for art's sake'.

In 1924, a government department wanted Regent Street rebuilt in the Renaissance style. Liberty's felt this style was not compatible with their image, preferring Tudor architecture. They compromised and built the shop fronting Regent Street as asked, but built a Tudor house on property at the rear. The Tudor building was built with the wood of two old man-of-war ships – HMS *Hindustan* and HMS *Impregnable*.

If you walk down Great Marlborough Street or Kingly Street you can see the outside of the Tudor building.

When you leave Liberty's, walk up Regent Street to Oxford Street.

If you go left, you will pass John Lewis, Debenhams, and Selfridges – which has the popular Miss Selfridge for young women and teenagers. All of these department stores have clothes, accessories and furnishings at reasonable prices. Your closest underground station, in this case, is Bond Street.

If you go right at Oxford Street, you will pass Peter Robinson and Marks and Spencer, two other department stores. The closest underground is Oxford Circus.

Did You Spot?

1. What was protruding from the Knight's boot?
2. How many carved chests there were?
3. What the boy and girl were holding?
4. What was crawling up the leaf?
5. What the painting of the two men was called?
6. The interests of the men by looking at the things on the shelves?
7. The unrecognizable thing at the bottom of the painting?

Do You Know?

8. How many times you can see the couple in the marriage painting? Why?
9. The instrument in the painting of the girls by Vermeer?
10. Nelson's Christian name?

Cardinal Wolsey

TOUR 18
The Hampton Court Palace of Cardinal Wolsey and Henry VIII

1 Hampton Court Palace, East Molesey, Surrey.
Tel. (01) 977 8441
British Rail: Hampton Court Station
Bus: 111, 131, 216, 267, 461. Green Lines: 715, 716, 718, 726
1 April–30 September: 09.30–18.00 Monday–Saturday; 11.00–18.00 Sunday
1 October–31 March: 09.30–17.00 Monday–Saturday; 14.00–17.00 Sunday
A ££, C £, P £
There are guided tours and also cassette tapes to listen to
Wheelchair/Shop/Restaurants/Toilet

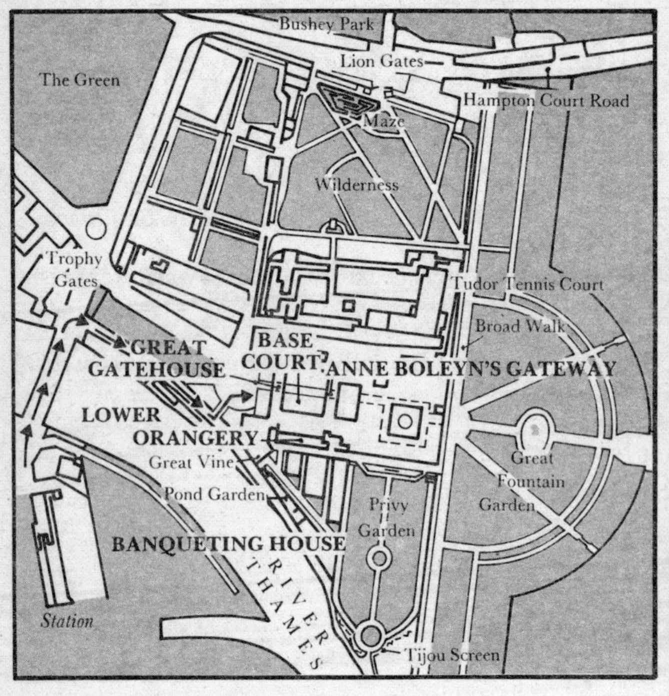

Bushey Park
Lion Gates
The Green
Hampton Court Road
Maze
Wilderness
Trophy
Gates
Tudor Tennis Court
Broad Walk
GREAT
GATEHOUSE
BASE
COURT
ANNE BOLEYN'S GATEWAY
LOWER
ORANGERY
Great Vine
Great
Fountain
Garden
Pond Garden
Privy
Garden
BANQUETING HOUSE
RIVER THAMES
Station
Tijou Screen

British Rail Hampton Court

Hampton Court Station is just across the river from the Palace. When you come out, walk to Hampton Court Way, go right, cross the bridge and go into the grounds.

11.00 Hampton Court Palace

As you approach Hampton Court, notice the faces of Roman emperors on the towers. They were made for Cardinal Wolsey (1475–1530). Henry VIII's (1491–1547) arms are under the oriel window.

Base Court

This court remains much as it was when it was built for Cardinal Wolsey. Look for the initials of Queen Elizabeth I (1533–1603) and the date of 1566. The apartment under the clock facing you is where it is thought Queen Anne Boleyn (1507–36) lived before she was taken to the Tower for execution. It may be why the gate is called Anne Boleyn's Gateway.

In the shop on your right, you can buy a guide book or other souvenirs. At the exit of the shop go to the ticket office where you can purchase tickets for the State Apartments.

Clock Court

The Court is named after the clock in the Tower – an astronomical clock made for King Henry VIII in 1540 – which indicates the time, the day of the month, number of days since the beginning of the year, phases of the moon, and the time of high water at London Bridge. As the King went often to the Tower by barge, this was useful information.

Go up the King's Staircase, built in 1700, which takes you to the King's Guardroom.

King's Guardroom

On the wall, you will see arms arranged in beautiful patterns, created for William III (1650–1702) – powder horns, pouches for shot, bayonets, swords, pistols, and saddle pistols, which were longer. You will also see lances of two sizes, the longer ones making pillars. Originally the lances were 10 feet longer, but were cut to this size in order to fit onto the wall. You will see how they were used when you look at two paintings in the third of Cardinal Wolsey's Rooms.

Wolsey's Room

Cardinal Wolsey did not live in these rooms. They were reserved for guests or members of his household. The walls have linen-fold wood panelling. There are various paintings in these rooms, one of which is of Erasmus (1466–1536), a philosopher, who was a great friend of Henry VIII. Wolsey's Closet, the only remaining personal room of his, is beautiful with a moulded ceiling and the original fireplace.

William and Mary's Rooms

You return through the King's Guardroom and go into the **First Presence Chamber**. Here is a chair of state of William III with its canopy. The carvings over the doors were done by Grinling Gibbons (1648–1721) in limewood. Now go through the **Second Presence Chamber**, the **Audience Chamber** with a chair of state, the **King's Drawing Room** and **William III's State Bedroom**. The next room is the **King's Dressing Room**, where King William really slept, and the **King's Writing Closet**. If you look into the mirror in the corner of the room, you will be able to see all the way back to the First Presence Chamber.

The **Queen's Gallery** is 80 feet long and has a beautiful marble chimneypiece and carvings by Grinling Gibbons.

In the **Queen's Bedroom** there is a bed made for George II (1683–1760) and Queen Caroline (1683–1737) when they were the Prince and Princess of Wales. As you go through the **Queen's Drawing**

Room, look out of the window at the cone-shaped trees, the canal, and the water fountain. In the **Queen's Audience Chamber** is a painting of Anne of Denmark (1574–1619), the wife of King James I (1566–1625), and one of Charles I (1600–1649) (the king who was executed on the orders of Oliver Cromwell, 1599–1658) when he was a young man. The room was the state reception room of the Prince and Princess of Wales during the reign of George I (1660–1727).

The **Public Dining Room** is so named because George II occasionally dined here in public. You can see a painting of Charles I with his Queen, Henrietta Maria (1609–69). You will now pass through the **Prince of Wales' Presence Chamber** and **Drawing Room.**

Next is the **Prince of Wales' Bedroom**, which contains the bed of Queen Anne (1665–1714). This magnificent bed was made for her in 1714 for use at Windsor Castle and was subsequently moved to Hampton Court. It has been restored to its former beauty by placing the original embroidered panels on new material woven in the same pattern as the bed's original material. The embroidery was done by 10–13-year-old girls living at the Hampton Orphanage.

Go over the **Prince of Wales' Staircase** to the **Queen's Private Chapel** and the **Queen's Bathing Closet.** Here you can see a basin inset to the wall with a tap. There is a view of Fountain Court from the window. Next is the **Private Dining Room** and another **Little Closet,** leading to the **Queen's Private Chambers** with another basin.

The **King's Private Dressing Room** leads to George II's **Private Chamber** and into the **Cartoon Gallery.** This room was designed by Christopher Wren (1632–1723) and is called the Cartoon Gallery because it contains copies of cartoons painted by

Raphael (1483–1520) which he submitted to the Vatican as designs for tapestries. In this room, you will see a painting of Henry VIII, his children, and Jane Seymour (c. 1509–37), who was the mother of his only son, Edward IV (1537–53). She died two weeks after Edward was born. In the corner of the painting you can see Henry's jester, Will Somers.

In the **Communication Gallery** you will see portraits of beautiful women of the court of Charles II.

You can then go through the **Cumberland Suite** – Georgian rooms with white and turquoise colours. Here you can see a painting of King Charles and Queen Henrietta dining in public.

As you walk into the **Haunted Gallery**, think of Catherine Howard (1520–42) who, tradition says, ran towards the Chapel to plead with King Henry. She is supposed to have been stopped by Henry's guard just before she reached the entrance. Catherine was imprisoned in the rooms where the Cumberland Suite is now located. Her ghostly screams have not been heard for about 100 years.

Go into the **Royal Chapel** – you enter the royal pew – where you will have a wonderful view of the ceiling and nave. It is magnificent with its blue fan-vaulted ceiling, painted with gold stars and cherubs playing pipes. Edward VI was baptized here and his mother, Jane Seymour, laid in state for three weeks before her burial.

The **Great Watching Chamber** is where King Henry VIII's special guard, six men, stood to guard his Presence Chamber and State Rooms, now destroyed. These men were specially armed with a cannon-type rifle. Look at the pillar to your left at the end of the room – the round object at the bottom is one of these rifles. There were only six made, and the other five are at the Tower of London.

The **Great Hall** was originally built by Wolsey, but improved by Henry VIII. The dais, a low platform at the end of the room, is where the table for the King and his guests was laid. Other people sat along both sides of the room. Notice the hearth-stone in front of the dais where a fire burned to warm the room. The stained glass is Victorian.

13.00 When you finish looking at the State Apartments, go out of the Palace and turn right to the Maze. See how long it takes you to find your way out again!

Then walk through the **Wilderness** to **Broad Walk** and the **Tudor Tennis Court**, which is not always open. As you go down Broad Walk you will see the **Great Fountain Garden**, which used to have thirteen fountains; now there is only one.

Walk into the **Privy Garden** and then on towards the river. Here you will see the beautiful wrought-iron screen made by Jean Tijou. Follow the river to the right to the **Banqueting House**, built by William III, and then to the **Great Vine**, which is past the **Pond Garden**. This vine was planted during the reign of George III (1730–1820).

Did You Spot?
1. The most common wood used by Grinling Gibbons for his carvings?
2. The name of Henry VIII's jester?
3. Who originally built Hampton Court?

Do You Know?
4. What dogs are named after a King?
5. The names of the six wives of Henry VIII?
6. When the astronomical clock was made?
7. The name of the Lord Protector after the execution of Charles I?

8. Who was Queen when the maze was planted?
9. What version of the Bible is named after a King?
10. What country George I came from?

TOUR 19
Toys, Cat Mummies and Viking Hoards

1 Pollock's Theatre and Toy Museum, 1 Scala
St, London W1. Tel. (01) 636 3452
☉ Goodge Street; Bus 14, 24, 29, 73
10.00–17.00 Monday–Saturday. *Closed*: Good Friday,
Easter Monday, Spring and Summer Bank Holidays,
24, 25 December
A £, C £, P £, S £; Shop

2 Paperchase, Tottenham Court Rd, London W1
☉ Goodge Street; Bus 14, 24, 29, 73
10.00–17.00 Monday–Saturday. *Closed*: Sunday

3 The British Library, Great Russell St, London
WC1. Tel. (01) 636 1544
☉ Tottenham Court Road, Goodge Street, Russell Square,
Holborn
Bus 14, 19, 22, 25, 38, 55
10.00–17.00 Monday–Saturday; 14.00–18.00 Sunday.
Closed: 24, 25, 26 December, 1 January, Good Friday,
1st Monday in May

4 The British Museum, Great Russell Street, London
WC1. Tel. (01) 636 1555
☉ Tottenham Court Road, Goodge Street, Russell Square,
Holborn
Bus 14, 19, 22, 25, 38, 55
10.00–17.00 Monday–Saturday; 14.30–18.00 Sunday.
Closed: 24, 25, 26 December, 1 January, Good Friday,
1st Monday in May
Wheelchair/Shop/Food/Toilet

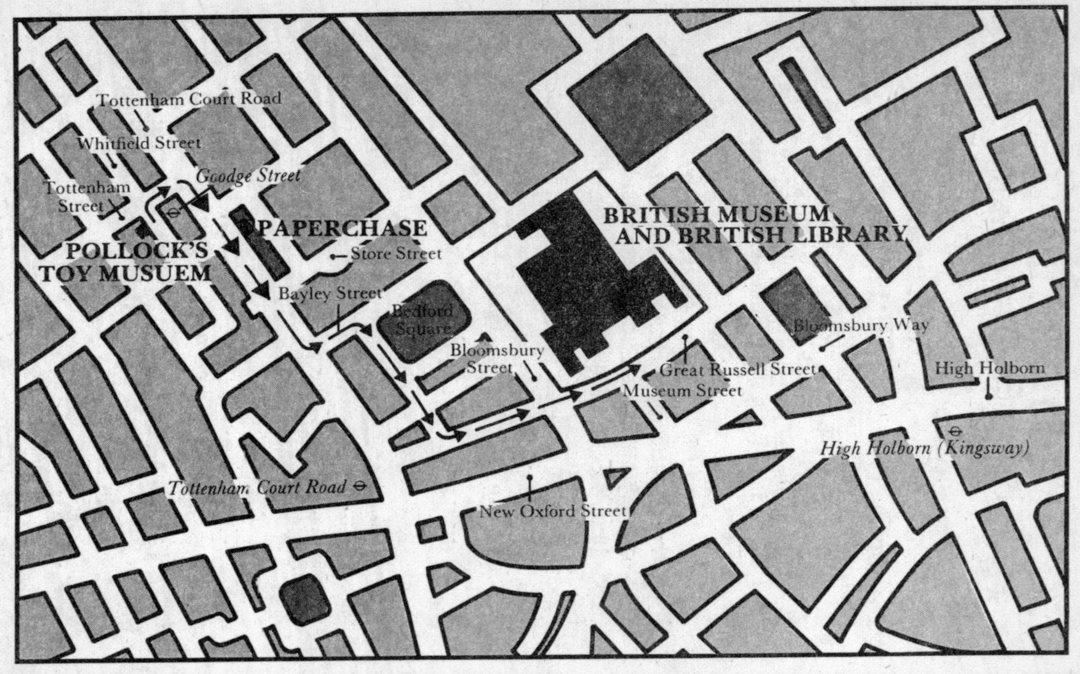

Tottenham Court Road
Whitfield Street
Tottenham Street
Goodge Street
POLLOCK'S TOY MUSUEM
PAPERCHASE
Store Street
Bayley Street
Bedford Square
Bloomsbury Street
BRITISH MUSEUM AND BRITISH LIBRARY
Bloomsbury Way
Great Russell Street
Museum Street
High Holborn
High Holborn (Kingsway)
Tottenham Court Road
New Oxford Street

⊖ Goodge Street

Pollock's is best suited for children aged 7–12. Younger children will find things of interest, but must be accompanied by an adult.

Either take a packed lunch or try to get something to eat after leaving the Pollock Museum.

When you leave Goodge Street Underground, you will come out on Tottenham Court Road. Go left, then turn left into Tottenham Street and go left again at Whitfield Street. You will see the entrance to Pollock's next to the Hope Pub.

11.00 Pollock's Theatre and Toy Museum

Through the door to the right, you will find toys made of wood, raffia, steel and baked bread-dough. There is a nut pig whose eyes, ears and tail move, and there are American Indian and Eskimo toys.

In **Room 1** you will see a large rocking-horse made in 1840, building bricks, and some very early Meccano.

In **Room 2** are all kinds of puppets and early Chad Valley toys.

In **Room 3** is a tiny wax doll which was hidden in a bouquet of flowers and presented to a child actor when he made his curtain call.

Room 4 has very old teddy bears and toy shops. There is a beautiful tea service complete with a kitchen range and pots and pans.

Room 5 has a nursery with an old fireplace and a bed full of dolls and teddy bears; there is also an old bath.

Room 6 is full of toy theatres, the oldest of which was made in 1820.

When you leave Pollock's, retrace your steps to Tottenham Court Road. Turn right and cross the road just after Goodge Street. Go into Paperchase.

12.00 Paperchase

Wander among this colourful world of paper in all shapes and sizes. You may want to buy a poster, writing paper, a lantern, hat, box, party invitation, mobile, stencil, a fan or a kite.

On leaving Paperchase, turn left down Tottenham Court Road. Cross Store Street and turn left into Bayley Street. Stay on the right side, walk past Bedford Square, and proceed straight to Great Russell Street.

This part of London is called Bloomsbury and gave its name to the Bloomsbury Group of artists and writers who lived in the area. You will see blue plaques on house fronts showing where famous people lived. University College London is slightly to the north.

Turn left into Great Russell Street. Pass André Deutsch Publishers on your left and the Trades Union Congress on your right. Cross Bloomsbury. In front of the Museum are various shops selling coins, old prints and books. The entrance is to your left.

The first door to the right leads into the British Library.

13.00 The British Library

In the British Library, you will find a large collection of written work of many famous people. You can see Samuel Pepys's (1633–1703) shorthand notes of a conversation he had with a lady, Jonathan Swift's (1667–1745) tiny writing, Jane Austen's (1775–1817) original manuscript of the last two chapters of *Persuasion*, Robert Scott's (1868–1912) last message, and Horatio Nelson's (1758–1805) last letter to Emma Hamilton (1761–1815).

There is a Book of Gospels written in 698 which is in excellent condition. You will see music written by Beethoven (1770–1827), Mozart (1756–91) and Handel (1685–1759). You will also see the Venerable Bede's (673–735) *History of England* and the Magna Carta, signed in 1215 by King John (1167–1216), which established the rule of law in England.

Turn left into **Room 32**, where you will find writing implements, book illustrations, and bindings and printing by William Caxton (1422–91) who printed Chaucer's *Canterbury Tales* in 1478.

13.00 The British Museum

When you get to the end of **Room 32**, go up the four sets of stairs. At the top go into **Room 53** (Anatolia and Iran).

Notice the baked clay coffin on the right side in case 17. Go through Rooms **52, 51, 50, 49** and then into **41**, an early Medieval room. In case 21 is a glass vase made in the 4th Century. When the glass was made it was coloured with manganese and a type of gold which causes the vase to appear green; but when a light is shone behind it, it turns red.

You will also see the Sutton Hoo Burial hoard. Because of the richness of the hoard, it is thought that these objects belonged to a King who lived about AD 600. Notice the drinking horns and the tubs. There is a copy of a cauldron and the suspension chain (pieces of it are in a cabinet).

Go back to the centre of Room 41 and into another Medieval room (**Room 42**). By the door, you will see a Viking hoard of silver coins, jewellery, buckles and other metal objects found in a chest in 1840.

On your left are the 12th Century Lewis Scandinavian chessmen made of walrus tusk. They were found on the Isle of Lewis off the coast of Scotland. On your right is a glittern, an early violin which may have belonged to Queen Elizabeth 1 (1533–1603).

As you go into **Room 44**, you will see a very early

clock made in the 1300s. The walk around the clock room takes you through the development of clocks, beginning with weight-driven ones. The clocks are all set at different minutes of the hour so that while you are there one or more will chime. They all make different sounds as some have one bell, while others have eight or nine. Look up at the top of the tall brass clock in the centre of the room and notice the figures on top. See if anything moves on the quarter-hour.

You will now go into **Room 45**, which contains items given by Lord Rothschild. Then go into **Room 46**, where you will find a red wax death-mask, jewellery, mementoes and silver. Turn into Room 41 (the Sutton Hoo Burial), and go into **Room 40** – Roman Britain, with pots, coins, tombs, wall decorations and jewellery. Walk through **Room 35** and veer to the left into **Room 68**, which contains Greek and Roman statues. Then go into **Room 69**, containing silver dishes, amphora for oil or wine, armour and statues of gladiators.

Go into **Room 70**, a room full of busts of famous Romans – the Emperors Caracalla (188–217), Marcus Aurelius (121–80), Titus (39–81), Claudius (10 BC–AD 54), Tiberius (42 BC–AD 37), Augustus (63 BC–AD 14) and Julius Caesar (100–44 BC). Then pass through **Rooms 71**, **72**, **73** and **59** and walk into **Room 61**.

Room 61 is full of Egyptian mummies and coffins. The first one you will see is called Ginger, because he has blondish hair. He is actually not a mummy; his body became dried through the heat of the sand. To the side of him, you will see a man who was buried in a basket in about 3000 BC. Look at the wall paintings and the painted coffins, both inside and out.

Room 60 is also full of mummies. The first mummy on the right has sandal-like shoes on his feet and the linen wrapping his body had been painted to show his

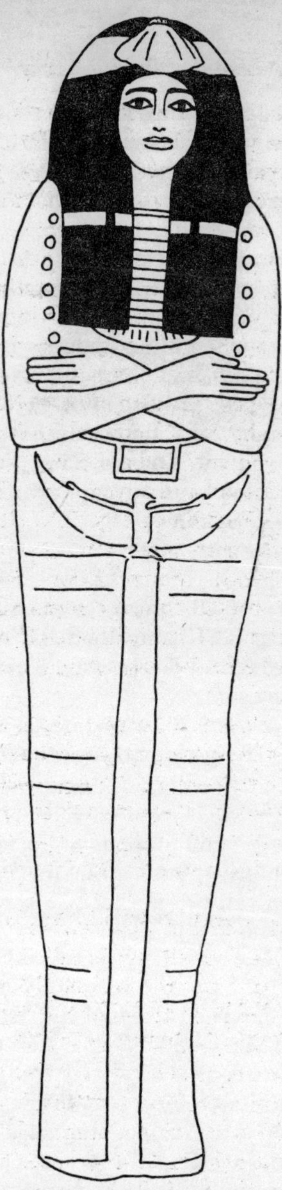

Inner coffin of Henutmehit, from
the British Museum

fingernails. There are mummies of babies, girls and boys, young men, ladies and older men, even of animals. One girl, called Cleopatra, daughter of Candace, died when she was 11. She has a comb, beads and remains of flowers.

Go back the way you came to the stairs and go down. When you reach the bottom, go right into **Room 25**.

Now you will walk past large Egyptian statues of gods, goddesses, and pharoahs. In exhibit 9 is a black head of Rameses VI (1172–1166 BC) and on the opposite side are Rameses I and II (1304–1237 BC). There are many heads of King Amenophis III (died 1380 BC). Look at the group of four marble statues of the Goddess Sakhmet.

On-your right, you will pass a famous stone discovered in 1799; the text is written in three different scripts, one of which was Greek. A Frenchman named Jean-François Champollion (1790–1832) made a break-through in deciphering hieroglyphics with the help of this stone.

When you get to the end of Room 25, turn left into the Shop. The main entrance to the Museum is at the other end.

The underground stations of Tottenham Court Road (Northern Line), Russell Square (Piccadilly), and Holborn (Central) are all about the same distance from the Museum.

Did You Spot?
1. Where Scott sent his last message from?
2. Whose death mask it is ?
3. The name of the famous stone which made it possible to begin to decipher hieroglyphics?

Do You Know?
4. What makes the ears, eyes and tail move on the nut pig?
5. Another name for a puzzle?
6. The name of the most famous puppet show?
7. The name of the King when the Magna Carta was signed?
8. Where gladiators fought?
9. What Anatolia is called now?
10. When they think the King buried with the Sutton Hoo hoard lived?

TOUR 20
Passion Fruit and Steam Engines

1 The Royal Botanical Gardens, Kew, Richmond-
upon-Thames, Surrey
◉ Kew Gardens (District Line); Bus 27, 65
Train Kew Bridge (Southern Railway from Waterloo)
Summer: Gardens 10.00–20.00; Houses 11.00–16.45
Winter: Gardens 10.00–16.00; Houses 11.00–16.00
Closed: Gardens 25 December, 1 January;
Houses Good Friday, 24, 25, 26 December, 1 January
Shop/Wheelchair/Toilet/Refreshments

2 Kew Palace, Royal Botanical Gardens, Kew,
Richmond-upon-Thames, Surrey. Tel. (01) 940 3221
11.00–17.30 Monday–Sunday
A £, C £; Shop/Food/Toilet

**3 Kew Bridge Engines Trust and Water
Supply Museum,** Green Dragon Lane, Kew,
Richmond-upon Thames, Surrey. Tel. (01) 568 4757
Train Kew Bridge; Bus 27, 65, 237, 267 (7 on Sundays)
11.00–17.00 Saturday and Sunday;
Closed: Monday–Friday
A ££, C £, P £, S ££; Shop/Food/Toilet

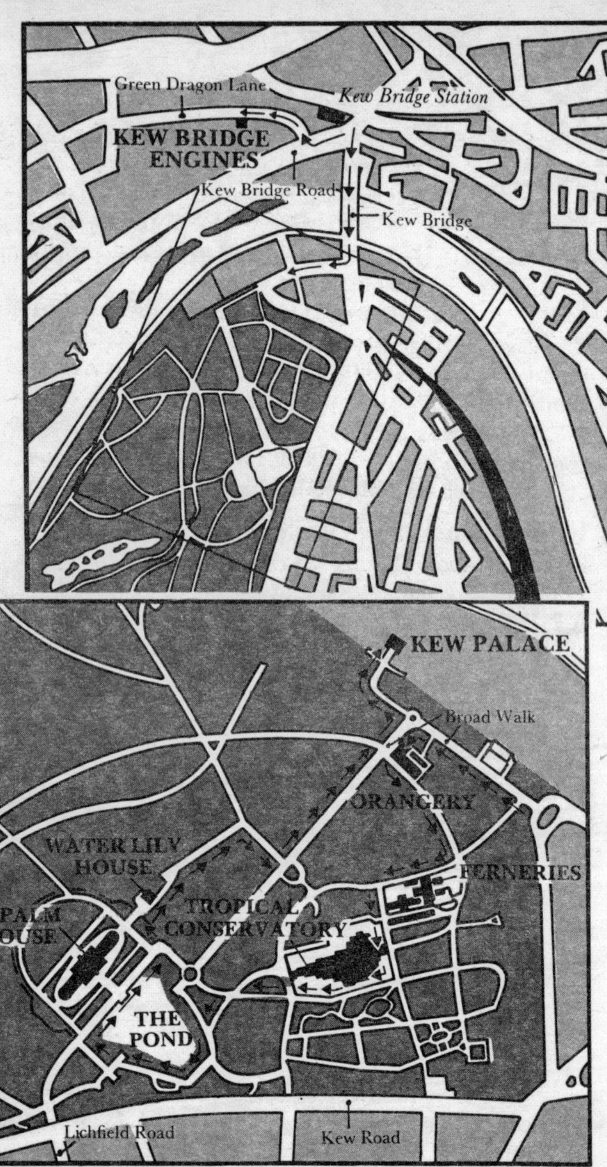

Green Dragon Lane
Kew Bridge Station
KEW BRIDGE ENGINES
Kew Bridge Road
Kew Bridge
KEW PALACE
Broad Walk
ORANGERY
FERNERIES
WATER LILY HOUSE
PALM HOUSE
TROPICAL CONSERVATORY
THE POND
Lichfield Road
Kew Road

Train Kew Bridge

When you leave the station, walk to Kew Bridge, cross and go right into the Main Entrance to Kew Gardens.

It is a beautiful place to eat a picnic lunch, and there are very nice pubs in Kew and a Refreshment Pavillion in the Gardens.

11.00 The Royal Botanical Gardens

The gardens were once two separate estates which belonged to members of the Royal Family. One estate belonged to George II (1683–1760) and Queen Caroline (1683–1737). They lived in Richmond Lodge, which is no longer in existence. Their son Frederick leased the Kew estate, and when he died, his wife, Augusta, started a botanical garden. They were the parents of George III (1738–1820), who inherited Richmond from his grandfather and Kew from his mother.

The Botanical Gardens first became famous during the life of George III, when rare plants began to arrive. In 1841, they were handed over to the State, and increased in size over the years by gifts of land from the Royal Family. In 1897 Queen Victoria (1819–1901) gave Queen Charlotte's Cottage and grounds to the State to celebrate her Diamond Jubilee.

As you walk from the main entrance, you will pass two majestic Indian Horse Chestnut trees. Continue walking until you see the side of the Orangery on your left. Walk to the entrance and go in. The Orangery was built by Princess Augusta in 1761; it contains a very good shop and an exhibition on the Garden.

When you leave the Exhibition, go left. Notice the strange-leaved plant to your right which is from South America. Go to the right at the next intersection.

In the buildings in this area, you will see very strange plants hanging from the ceiling. There are several ponds with fish swimming about and plants overhanging the edges. Notice the many shades of green.

There are tropical plants that flower throughout the year, the same types as can be bought as house plants. There is a pineapple plant, orchids growing on a dead tree, African violets, and carnivorous plants.

There are also plants from the desert which have to store water in order to survive. There is an *Agave sisalana* from which we get sisal for making ropes.

In the new conservatory, you will be able to see a mangrove swamp, a Mohave desert diorama, and an underground viewing area for the aquaria.

Now walk to the lake for a rest and to enjoy the scenery.

Then go left to the Museum. Inside is a very interesting model of an Indigo factory in India. There are exhibitions: of bead necklaces, some of which are poisonous; plant foods and medicines; trees and their products, such as bark, wax, oil, gums and resins; arrow poisons and rubber.

Go out of the Museum to the left and walk to the Palm House. On the way, you will see copies of the Queen's Beasts which were outside Westminster for Queen Elizabeth II's coronation.

The **Palm House** was built in 1844–8. Here you can see banana, cotton, rubber, cocoa plants, cycads (which are related to plants which lived over 100 million years ago), and ornamental plants.

Go left and then right to the very steamy **Water Lily House**. You will see a lily with leaves as big as a table. There are also luffa, sweet potato, papyrus, bottle gourd and sugar-cane plants.

When you leave, turn left and walk alongside the house. At the end of this path, turn right, then turn

left on to Broad Walk. Walk straight until you come
to a circular flower bed and go left to Kew Palace.

12.00 Kew Palace

Kew Palace was built in 1631 for Samuel Fortrey. It
was used by George III as an annex to Kew House
until 1802 when Kew House was pulled down. It has
the air of a family home. The Duke of Clarence (later
King William IV, 1765–1837) and Edward, Duke
of Kent (1767–1820), who was the father of Queen
Victoria, had their double wedding here in the drawing room.

Walk back to the circular flower bed and out of the
main entrance. Go back across the bridge and turn
left into Kew Bridge Road. Cross and go down Green
Dragon Lane to Kew Bridge Engines.

13.00 Kew Bridge Engines Trust and Water Supply Museum

Inside is the hissing of steam and huge engines which
actually work (according to a fixed timetable – not at
the same time). You will see a beam engine built in
1820, which is the oldest one there, a Compound
Rotative engine, a 90-inch engine, which is the largest
beam in the world, and a 100-inch single-cylinder
beam engine (the beam weighs 50 tons). Don't forget
to see the forge near the refreshment area.

Did You Spot?
1. The fern hanging from the ceiling with the funny name? What is it called?
2. The Queen's beasts? How many are there?

Do You Know?
3. A famous naval captain whose ships brought back specimens for the Garden?
4. What 'carnivorous' means?
5. What indigo is used for?
6. What gum arabic is used for?
7. What part of the plant is the spice cinnamon?
8. What part of the plant is a clove?
9. Where tea originally came from?
10. What name describes a man who uses a forge?

TOUR 21
Windsor Castle and Eton Village

1 Windsor Castle, Windsor
British Rail from Paddington and Waterloo; Green Line
Bus from Victoria.
Castle Precincts: 10.00 until an hour before sunset
Closed: During special functions
Queen Mary's Dolls' House:
End March–End October: 10.30–17.00 Monday–Saturday;
13.00–17.00 Sunday
End October–End March: 10.30–15.00 Monday–Saturday;
Closed: Sunday
A £, C £, P £, S £; Toilet/Shop
The State Apartments
End March–End October: 10.30–17.00 Monday–Saturday;
13.30–17.00 Sunday
End October–End March: 10.30–15.00 Monday–Saturday;
Closed: Sunday
A ££, C £
St George's Chapel
10.45–15.45 Monday–Saturday; 14.00–15.45 Sunday.
Closed: January
A ££, C £, P £

Note: The State Apartments are only open when the
Queen is not in residence. The times are varied, but
generally they are closed two weeks before Easter until
the beginning of May, most of June, and the last three
weeks in December

**2 Madame Tussaud's Royalty and Empire
Exhibition,** Windsor. Tel. 0753 857837
British Rail from Paddington and Waterloo; Green Line
Bus from Victoria
Royalty and Empire Exhibition: 09.30–17.30 Daily; A
££, C ££, P ££ Family of 2 Adults and 2 children ££££

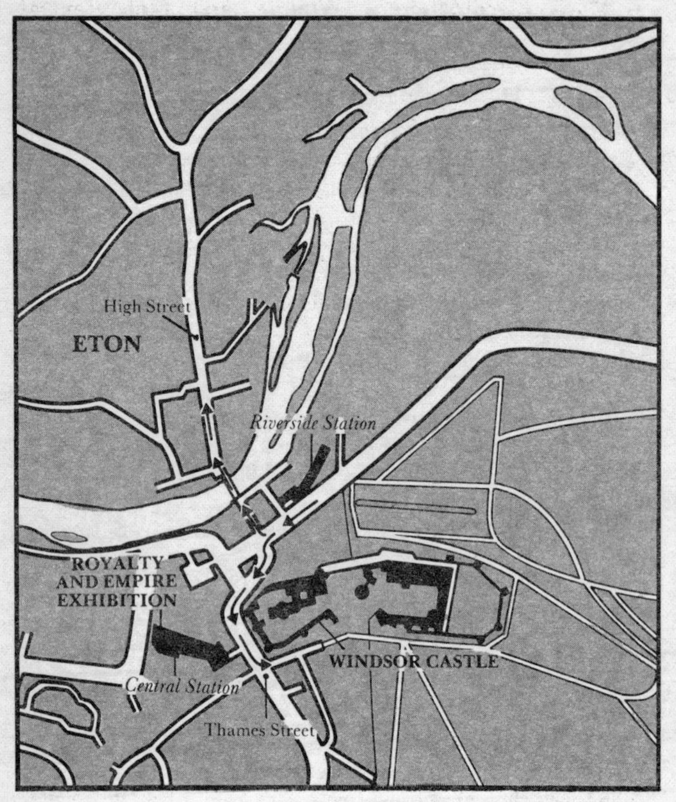

High Street
ETON
Riverside Station
ROYALTY
AND EMPIRE
EXHIBITION
Central Station
Thames Street
WINDSOR CASTLE

Train Waterloo to Windsor and Eton Riverside Station; leaves slightly past the hour and half-hour.

Train Paddington to Windsor and Eton Central, change at Slough; leaves close to the hour and half-hour.

The train journey lasts about an hour.

If you arrive at the Riverside Station, cross the street in front of the station and then cross the road to the left. Turn right and walk straight, turning with the road towards the Castle.

Go past Chapter Mews and the Theatre Royal. Have a look at the castle – the wall and towers were built in the 13th Century. Look at the tower with the conical roof. Do you see anything unusual in one of the windows?

If you arrive at Windsor and Eton Central, go out of the station and to the right. You will see the street leading to the Castle.

11.00 Windsor Castle

Go in through Henry VIII's Gate and just before you pass through, look up to see the three holes above you. These allowed defenders to pour boiling oil or water down on anyone attempting to break through the portcullis (an iron gate which could be lowered and raised).

You are now in the Lower Ward. You can see St George's Chapel in front of you and to your left, the parade ground where the guards are changed in winter, and a sentry box.* You can also see Horseshoe Cloister, built of red brick and timber.

On the right and slightly behind you are the lodgings of the Military Knights, a foundation created by King Edward III (1312–77) in the same year that he established the Order of the Garter. The aim of the

* Refer to Tour 4 to find out which guards are changing.

foundation was to provide living accommodation for retired officers who had served with distinction.

Look beyond the Chapel and you will see the Round Tower. The mound it is sitting on was made by William the Conqueror (1028–87) and the tower, built by Henry II (1113–98), was the main fortification of the castle.

At the upper end of the houses is the Henry III (1207–72) Tower. This tower, the houses below it and the next tower, the Mary Tudor Tower, are all 13th and 14th Century, and the yellow stone houses are 16th Century.

First, go into Horseshoe Cloister, which was built by Edward IV (1442–83) in the 15th Century. It contained accommodation for Priest-Vicars or Clergy, and now houses male singers of the choir and the Sacristans (assistants to the Verger). Notice the pattern of wood inset in the red bricks.

To get your ticket, go out of the Cloisters and walk round to the left. Then go into St George's Chapel.

St George's Chapel

In 1348, Edward III founded the College of St George at Windsor as the home of college priests who would pray for the souls of members of the Royal Family. He founded the chivalric Most Noble Order of the Garter in the same year and the college became its spiritual home.

When Edward IV came to power after his defeat of the Lancastrian Henry VI, he had land cleared to the west of Edward III's Chapel and began work on one which was eventually to be his tomb and chantry.

You can buy a plan of the Chapel quite cheaply which will give you a brief description of the important things in it.

You will see the tombs of the following:

Henry VI (1421–71). Henry VI became King when he was nine months old. He was an ineffectual ruler, but was keenly interested in the arts and learning, founding Eton College and King's College, Cambridge. He was murdered while at prayers in the Tower of London. Richard III (1452–85) was responsible for bringing his body to Windsor for reburial in 1484. Every year on the anniversary of his death, students from Eton and King's College say special prayers and then lay lilies and white roses on his tomb.

Edward IV (1442–83) and his Queen, Elizabeth Woodville (1437–92). The wrought-iron gates were made in 1482 and are considered to be the finest medieval ironwork in the country. Notice the stone window above the gates. This window belonged to one of three rooms which were above the tomb for chantry priests to use while praying for the King's soul. In 1789, while the paving in the north aisle was being repaired, an opening in the vault was found and the coffins of the King and Queen were discovered and opened. They found that Edward IV was 6′ 4″ tall and had chestnut hair. The opening was closed with the black marble slab and Edward IIII written in gold letters. His two sons (Edward V and Richard) were thought to have been murdered by the order of their uncle, Richard III.

Henry VIII (1491–1547), who is buried with Jane Seymour (1509–37), mother of his only son, Edward VI. Henry was the first King after Edward III to realize the importance of a navy. He used money wrested from the monasteries on their dissolution to help finance a fleet, which was the beginning of the English Navy. The *Mary Rose* (1545), his flagship, has now been recovered from the sea and can be seen at Portsmouth.

Charles I (1600–1649), who was executed outside the Banqueting House on Whitehall. The date for his death is based on the old style of dating in which the New Year started on 25 March.

Edward VII (1841–1910) and Queen Alexandra (1844–1925) of Denmark. Edward VII did not become King until he was 60 years old. Queen Victoria excluded him from affairs of state, but he eventually became a popular ruler and helped to keep peace in Europe.

King George V (1865–1936) and Queen Mary (1867–1953). George V was the second son of Edward VII; his elder brother Albert Victor was to be King but died. He changed the Royal Family name from Saxe-Coburg-Gotha to Windsor. The doll's house you will see was made for Queen Mary.

King George VI (1895–1952). George VI succeeded to the throne in 1936 on the abdication of his elder brother, Edward VIII. He was the father of Queen Elizabeth II.

George III (1738–1820) was King when England lost the American Colonies. From 1780 onwards, he suffered bouts of insanity caused by a disease called porphyria and was completely insane by 1811.

George IV (1762–1830) became Regent in 1811 because of George III's insanity. He secretly married Maria Fitzherbert, but the marriage was annulled because he was under-age. He then married Caroline of Brunswick, but separated from her after the birth of a daughter. He was not a popular king. In the Urswick Chantry, you will see the memorial to his daughter, Charlotte, who died in childbirth.

William IV (1765–1837) was known as the Sailor King or Silly Billy. He served in the Royal Navy for twelve years, and had ten illegitimate children before he married at the age of 53. He then had two daughters, who unfortunately died at early ages. On his death, he was succeeded by Queen Victoria.

You will come out into a passage and go past a painting of Edward III (1312–77) and one of his swords. There is also an alms box made in the 1440s for pilgrims to leave donations in.

You will pass narrow, winding stairs and the red East Door and then go into **Dean's Cloister**. This was built in the 1300s and is considered to be the earliest cloistered college in England. If it is open, go into Canons' Cloister, which was also built in the 1300s.

Now go into the Galilee Porch and left into the **Albert Memorial Chapel**, which was contructed by Henry VII on the site of the chapel built by Henry III in the 1200s. Cardinal Wolsey was going to use it for his tomb, but his fall from power put an end to that dream. When Prince Albert died, Queen Victoria restored the Chapel to perpetuate his memory. There is a cenotaph (empty tomb) of Prince Albert, whose tomb is at Frogmore. Buried here are Prince Leopold (1853–84), son of Queen Victoria and Prince Albert, and Albert Victor (1864–92), elder son of Edward VII and Queen Alexandra.

Go out and walk to the left to the Norman Gate. This was built in the 1300s. Walk to the ticket office and buy tickets for the State Apartments and Dolls' House.

The **Dolls' House** was built by the famous architect Sir Edwin Landseer Lutyens (1869–1944) in the 1920s, for Queen Mary. It has four floors, a basement, a formal garden and a wine cellar, and is suitably furnished for a palace. There are also displays of dolls and doll furniture.

Go to the **State Apartments**.

As you go up the **Grand Staircase**, you will see a statue of George IV and a suit of armour of Henry VIII. There are two knights on their chargers. All about are displays of breast plates, swords, spears, lances, and helmets. This staircase was built for Queen Victoria in 1866.

In the **Grand Vestibule** is a statue of Queen Victoria and displays of arms, a sedan chair and other interesting items, including the armour of the King of Mysore of 1799, who fought under the Duke of Wellington (1769–1851), and the ball shot which killed Lord Nelson (1758–1805).

Now go into the **Waterloo Chamber**. This was once a courtyard, but George IV had it covered over and made into a banqueting chamber to celebrate Wellington's victory; the banquet is held on 18 June every year. There are paintings of all the monarchs, statesmen and soldiers involved in Napoleon's defeat. You will see Frederick, the Duke of York. Do you remember a song about him?

Now you will see the **Garter Throne Room**, which George IV had constructed for the ceremonies of the Knights of the Garter (these occur in June), and the **Grand Reception Room**, where the guests who are attending the Waterloo Banquet on 18 June gather.

St George's Hall was built by Edward III, and George IV doubled it in size. You will see paintings of Monarchs of England from James I to George IV. In the **Queen's Guard Chamber** are displays of arms. This is where a person wishing to have an audience with the Queen was met by the Yeoman of the Guard before being ushered into the **Queen's Presence Chamber**. George III gave concerts in here. Then go into the **Queen's Audience Chamber**, where the Queen would receive her visitors.

In the **Queen's Ball Room** (named for Queen Catherine of Braganza, wife of Charles II) are several interesting paintings. One is 'The Three Youngest Daughters' of George III, by the American artist John Singleton Copley (1738–1815); the other is of the five eldest children of Charles I by Sir Anthony Van Dyke (1599–1641).

The **Queen's Drawing Room** contains paintings of Elizabeth I (1533–1603), her sister Mary Tudor (1516–58), their brother Edward VI (1537–53), Charles I (1600–1649), Mary II (1662–94), Charles II

(1630–85) when young, William III (1650–1702) when Prince of Orange, and Henry VIII (1491–1547).

Now you will pass through the **King's Closet** and into the **King's Dressing Room**, where you will see the famous painting by Van Dyke of King Charles I in three poses. This was painted so that an Italian sculptor (Bernini, 1598–1680) could fashion a bust of the King without either of them having to travel.

Now walk across a bridge over the entrance and leave the apartments. Go out of the Castle.

13.00 Windsor is full of pubs of restaurants.

When you come out of the Castle, cross the street and turn down the side of the Horse and Groom Pub.

To your right, you will see Market Cross House, built in 1771. Notice how it leans to one side. Walk round to the front door and go inside to see how low the ceilings are.

Then cross the High Street at the traffic lights and go right. Turn left into the Great Western Railway Station, where you will see a carriage waiting for the Queen, as well as hear a newspaper boy shouting the headlines of 1897. Go through the station to the ticket office of Madame Tussaud's Royalty and Empire Exhibition.

14.00 Madame Tussaud's Royalty and Empire Exhibition

You will walk along a fence showing old advertisements and then enter a room where Abdul Karim, a secretary of Queen Victoria, sits. Then go into the Royal Waiting Room, where you will see Queen Victoria and the Prince and Princess of Wales (King Edward VII and Queen Alexandra). The Queen is awaiting the arrival of her favourite daughter Victoria, Princess Royal and Dowager Empress of Prussia.

GREAT WESTERN RAILWAY

TIME TABLE OF THE TRAIN

CONVEYING

HER MAJESTY THE QUEEN

AND SUITE

FROM WINDSOR TO PADDINGTON

ON

MONDAY, JUNE 21st, 1897

WINDSOR . . . . depart 12·0 noon.
PADDINGTON . . . arrive 12·35 p.m.

from 'Royalty and Empire',
Windsor

Now go out and look into the train, where you will see the Empress with her son Prince Henry of Prussia, the Grand Duke Serge, the Grand Duchess Elizabeth of Russia, and Princess Irene of Hesse (both granddaughters of Queen Victoria).

Go up the stairs and walk round the Royal Parade, where you will see Queen Victoria coming out with her daughter, followed by the Princess of Hesse restraining a young cousin; behind them is the Prince of Wales and Prince Henry of Prussia. Seventy Coldstream Guards are giving the Royal Salute and presenting arms, and the Coldstream band is playing the National Anthem of Germany. You will also see the Maharajah Sir Partab Singh and Arthur, Duke of Connaught, Queen Victoria's youngest son.

You will now go into a theatre where you will see photographs giving you an idea of the world as it was during Queen Victoria's Jubilee; you will also see a narrated scene with moving wax figures of Queen Victoria, Prince Albert and famous people of the time – Charles Dickens, Florence Nightingale, and Benjamin Disraeli.

Exit through the shop and you will find yourself in the train station.

You can take a train from here to Paddington Station in London, changing at Slough. Paddington serves the Bakerloo, Metropolitan, Circle and District lines.

Or you can go back to the High Street and go left. At the William IV Pub, cross the street and go straight down Thames Street, past Wren's Old House Hotel and across the bridge. You are now in Eton.

16.00 Eton

Eton High Street is full of old houses and antique shops. You will see a house with its windows only several inches from the pavement; notice the supports under two other windows. You will pass a building called the Cock Pit, which was sold in 1410 by the Dean of Windsor to a man called John Strugnell. If you continue walking on this street, you will arrive at Eton College, founded by Henry VI in 1440.

If you want to return by way of Waterloo Station, just turn left after crossing the bridge on leaving Eton.

Did You Spot?

1. Something in a window in the tower with the conical roof?
2. Whose statue is standing in front of Windsor Castle?
3. What the feet of Napoleon III's son are resting on?
4. How many place settings are on the table?
5. What is inset into the pavement between the Great Western Railway and the Bridge?

Do You Know?

6. What jubilee Queen Victoria was celebrating?
7. The name of the man who built the Great Western Railway?
8. Which guards are guarding Windsor Palace?
9. The mystical animal St George is supposed to have fought?
10. The song about the Duke of York?

Statuette of Wellington, from
Apsley House

TOUR 22
The Iron Duke and King Charles's Pensioners

1 Apsley House, 149 Piccadilly, London W1.
Tel. (01) 499 5676
⊖ Hyde Park Corner; Bus 19, 30, 73
10.00–18.00 Tuesday–Thursday, Saturday;
14.30–18.00 Sunday
Closed: Monday and Friday
A £, C £, P £, S £; Wheelchair/Shops/Toilet

2 The Royal Hospital, Chelsea, Royal Hospital
Road, London SW3. Tel. (01) 730 0161
⊖ Sloane Square; Bus 11, 22, 39, 137
10.00–14.00 and 14.00–16.00 Monday–Saturday;
14.00–16.00 Sunday
Closed: Sunday mornings except for those attending
church
Museum is *closed* Sundays from 1 October to 30 March
and on Bank Holidays
Shop/Toilet

If a party of people are going you must write to the Adjutant
and make arrangements for a visit. You will be given a time
and assigned a pensioner to guide you round. Allow 4–6
weeks. If you go as a family or just one or two people a guide
is not necessary, but you can only visit the Great Hall,
Chapel, State Apartments and Museum. The Hospital is
the residence of many people and although they welcome
visitors, they ask that children do not run about.

3 The National Army Museum, Royal Hospital
Road, London SW3. Tel. (01) 730 0717
⊖ Sloane Square; Bus 11, 22, 39, 137
10.00–17.30 Monday–Saturday; 14.00–17.30 Sunday
Closed: Good Friday, 1st Monday May, 24, 25, 26
December, 1 January
Wheelchair/Shop/Toilet

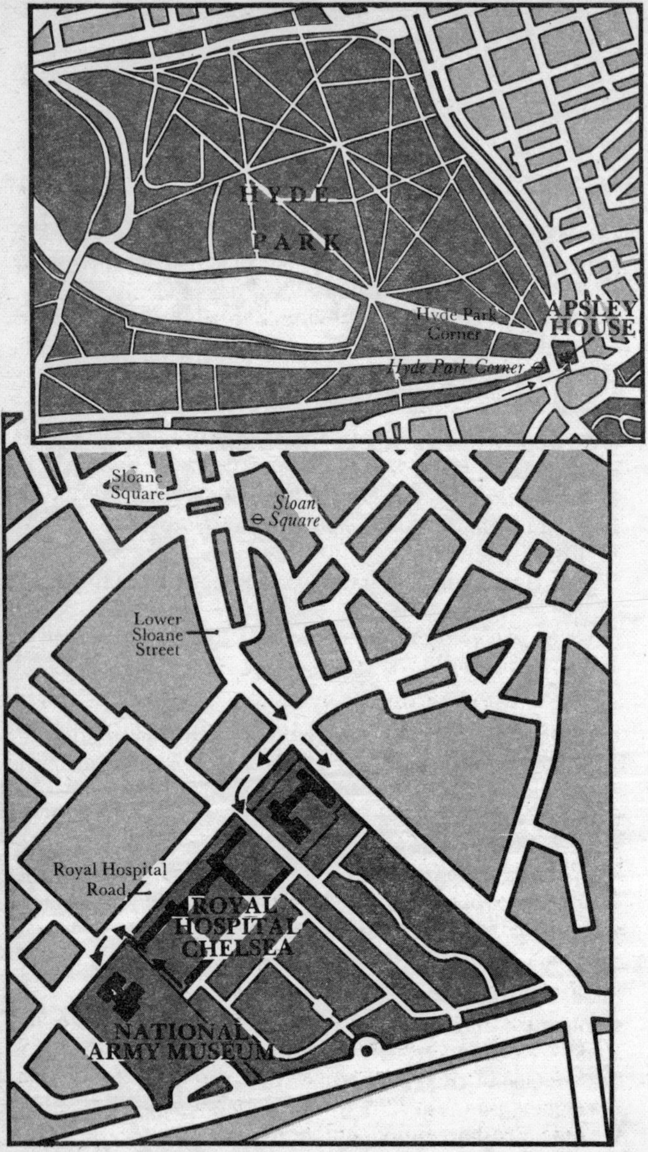

HYDE PARK
Hyde Park Corner
Hyde Park Corner
APSLEY HOUSE
Sloane Square
Sloan Square
Lower Sloane Street
Royal Hospital Road
ROYAL HOSPITAL CHELSEA
NATIONAL ARMY MUSEUM

⊖ Hyde Park Corner

Try to bring a packed lunch on this tour as there are not many eating places.

When you go through the ticket barrier go to the exit marked for the Wellington Museum. At the top of the steps do an about-turn and walk up past the triple-arched screen. Apsley House will be on your left.

The Duke of Wellington was born Arthur Wellesley in 1769 in Dublin. He joined the Army and was posted to India. By the time he was 30 years old, he had been made Governor of Mysore. He liberated Portugal and Spain from French rule in 1814 and, with General Blücher (1742–1819) of Prussia, defeated Napoleon in 1814, and once again at the Battle of Waterloo in 1815. He held many important posts in English Government: Prime Minister, Foreign Secretary and Commander in Chief of the British Army.

11.30 Apsley House

In the entrance **Hall**, you will see two ceremonial robes worn by the Duke, and some flags presented by Napoleon (1769–1821) to French Departments in 1815.

Go through the beautiful doors into the **Plate and China Room**. Here you will see swords, medals, batons and snuff boxes. There is a dinner service with a centre-piece that is 17 feet long. Napoleon gave this service to the Empress Josephine (1763–1814) as a present on their divorce, but she didn't want it. It was given to the Duke of Wellington by Louis XVIII of France (1755–1824). There is also a pair of duelling pistols. Have a close look at the candelabra made for the Duke in 1816 and presented to him by the City of London. At the base of each are soldiers of different regiments and below the soldiers are their hats, muskets, drums, cannon and balls.

Now go back to the entrance Hall and into the
Inner Hall. It contains busts of the Duke of Wellington and several uniforms.

Near the **Staircase** is a statue of Napoleon in the
classical Greek posture. Napoleon commissioned this
statue from Antonio Canova (1757–1822), an Italian
sculptor, but when it was finished he decided he didn't
like it and put it out of the way in the Louvre.

Go up the stairs and into the left room, which is
called the **Piccadilly Drawing Room**. It was
designed by Robert Adam (1728–92) and when first
built would have had pale green walls like the walls
of the staircase. There is a beautiful arched ceiling
and in the room are gold silk walls, chairs and
paintings, including one by Brueghel the Elder
(1525–69). Pay particular attention to the painting
'Chelsea Pensioners Reading the Waterloo Despatch'
by Sir David Wilkie (1785–1841) in 1822 after the
Battle of Waterloo. You can see the Despatch in the
basement.

The next room is the **Portico Drawing Room**.
There are paintings of William Pitt (1759–1806),
Napoleon and his sister Pauline, and his wife the
Empress Josephine.

The **Waterloo Gallery** was built for the grand
dinners the Duke held every year on the anniversary
of the Battle of Waterloo, to which he invited the
officers who fought the battle under his command.
There are very tall candelabra, a present from the
Emperor Nicholas I of Russia (1796–1855). Many of
the paintings were captured during a battle in 1813
in Spain and presented to the Duke by the King of
Spain. Notice the parquet flooring up to the carpet,
the ceiling patterns of gilt plaster and white, and the
centre dome. The carpet is a copy of the carpets which
were in the house when the Duke was alive. There is
a painting of the Duke of Wellington by a famous
Spanish painter which the Duke didn't like at all.

There are also paintings of Mary Tudor (1516–58) and King Charles I (1600–1649). When the shutters are closed over the windows at night, the mirrors on them reflect the light in the room. It must have been beautiful with the sparkling of candlelight.

The chandelier in the **Yellow Drawing Room** was made in 1830. The bust of the dancer was made by the sculptor Antonio Canova. He gave this bust to the Duke in thanks for his efforts to have works of art returned to Rome which the French had taken to Paris when Napoleon was in power.

In the **Striped Drawing Room**, you will see paintings of what the room looked like in 1852 and of the military men who served with the Duke.

The Dining Room. The dining room table is very long indeed and has to be to hold the centrepiece of the Portuguese Service. The table and chairs were used by the Duke of Wellington for the Waterloo Dinners, and would be moved to the Waterloo Gallery. The centrepiece of the service shows the Four Continents paying tribute to the armies of Britain, Portugal and Spain. Originally there were garlands of silk flowers in the hands of the dancers.

You will now go through the **Hallway**, where you will see presentation pieces, and then down to the bottom of the staircase. You will see steps at the back of the staircase, and a painting of the 7th Duke of Wellington hanging on the wall.

If you go down these stairs, you will find campaign maps on the walls; one was filled in during the battle with the positions of the troops. There is also an engraving of the Duke of Wellington with Lord Nelson.

You will go past cartoons of the Duke. There are invitations issued to watch the funeral cortége as it went on its route and a Panorama of Wellington's Funeral which was published the year after he died. It was a very grand affair, as you can see.

12.30 If you have bought a packed lunch, you could eat it in Hyde Park. When you are ready to carry on, walk back in the direction of the Underground, pass it and go down the Pedestrian Subway. Go right at the sign saying 'South side of Knightsbridge'. Carry on round, passing another exit before emerging from the subway. Walk to the fourth bus stop in the row. Take Bus 137 to Chelsea.

Get off the bus at the stop just past Royal Hospital Road. Cross the road (Lower Sloane Street) and go down Royal Hospital Road to the London Gate entrance of the Royal Hospital – it is just past the cemetery.

14.00 ## The Royal Hospital, Chelsea

The Royal Hospital was founded by Charles II (1630–85) for the welfare of veterans of the regular army who were unfit for duty after 20 years' service, or because of wounds. The site was chosen by Christopher Wren (1632–1723) and he designed the hospital. Figure Court is the most complete Court left of his design.

Go into the grounds at London Gate and walk straight ahead. The Museum will be to your left.

Museum

Inside is a small shop selling souvenirs of the hospital, including some things made by the pensioners themselves.

In the same room, you will find many things related to the life of the Duke of Wellington. The oak table in front of the door is the one the Duke's coffin was laid on for his Lying in State at the Royal Hospital. There are several engravings showing the Lying in State, the crowds straining to get in (people were injured), and the funeral in St Paul's. There is an invitation to the Lying in State and several paintings of the Duke showing people where the Battle of Waterloo took place.

In the Museum itself, you will see information on the origin of the hospital. As you can see in the large engraving, the hospital grounds extended to the river with steps down to it. There are pictures of Nell Gwynne (1650–87), William (1650–1702) and Mary (1662–94), Charles II, James II (1633–1701) and his Queen and Christopher Wren.

There is a washstand from the Secretary's Office of 1820, paintings of pensioners, uniforms, a drum, and models of pensioners. There is also a big display of medals.

Go out of the Museum to the right and then turn left, walking across **Light Horse Court**, through the passage and into the next court, **Figure Court**. Turn left down the side of the Court, walk to the last door on the left and go in. It is just possible that the Council Chamber will be open to visitors. If so, there will be a notice. If not, return to the top of the Court and turn left.

Walk to the main entrance in the centre of the Court and go in. On the left is the **Great Hall**. This is where the pensioners eat their meals. There are paintings of George II (1683–1760) and Queen Caroline (1683–1737), and of John, Duke of Marlborough (1650–1722). Go out and into the **Chapel**, where there will be a pensioner to tell you about it.

Come out into the Figure Court and turn right. Walk into the **College Court** and out into the street at the end. Turn right and walk out of the Hospital grounds. Turn left.

It is only a few steps to the National Army Museum, which will be on your left. You will see a tank outside.

16.00 The National Army Museum

The National Army Museum is very modern, well laid-out and full of information on how the British

Army has developed since the 1400s. Numbers on the exhibits or arrows on the floor usually indicate where to move on to the next exhibit.

The first exhibit is the **Weapons Gallery**, which takes you through the development of weaponry from the bow and musket. There are working models of guns to show you how a natch lock, wheel lock, and flintlock work. There are swords, carbines, breach-loading guns, revolving cylinders, Maxims and Hotch-kiss weapons.

The second exhibit is on the Story of the Army, Parts I and II. The story starts with Cromwell's Army and includes various types of uniform, paintings of battles, the cloak that Colonel James Wolfe (1791–1823) was wrapped in on his death, uniforms and equipment of Gurkhas, a flute case and drum, the skeleton of Napoleon's favourite horse, a magnificent gun captured in India, and a head-dress from the Boxer Movement.

Part II has exhibits of soldiers in working situations – in trenches, a machine-gun nest, in an office, working radios, etc.

The **Uniform Gallery** has displays of uniforms of different regiments over many years, complete with hats, caps and helmets.

To get to Sloane Square, turn right when leaving the Museum and walk to Lower Sloane Road. Cross and turn left. Walk to Sloane Square, turn right and you will see the Underground in front of you.

Did You Spot?

1. The animal hanging from the Spanish Order of the Golden Fleece?
2. The name of the dinner service given to Wellington by Louis XVIII?
3. What Napoleon's statue is holding in his hand?
4. What two items have dropped to the ground near the table in the 'Chelsea Pensioners Reading the Wellington Despatch'?
5. The name of the Spanish artist who painted the picture of Wellington which he didn't like?
6. The length of the Portuguese Service centrepiece?
7. The name of Napoleon's horse?
8. What fur the head-dress is made from which was worn in the Boxer Movement?

Do You Know?

9. Where the Duke of Wellington's body lay in state at the Hospital?
10. Where Colonel Wolfe died?

TOUR 23
The Boys in Blue

1 The Battle of Britain Museum, Grahame Park
Way, Hendon, London NW9.
⊖ Colindale; Bus 79 (along Edgware Road)
10.00–18.00 Monday–Saturday; 14.00–18.00 Sunday;
Closed: Good Friday, 1st Monday May,
24, 25, 26 December, 1 January
A £, C £; Wheelchair/Shop/Food/Toilet

2 The Royal Air Force Museum, Grahame Park
Way, Hendon, London NW9. Tel. (01) 205 2266
⊖ Colindale; Bus 79 (along Edgware Road)
10.00–18.00 Monday–Saturday; 14.00–18.00 Sunday;
Closed: Good Friday, 1st Monday May,
24, 25, 26 December, 1 January
Wheelchair/Shop/Food/Toilet

3 The Bomber Command Museum, Grahame
Park Way, Hendon, London NW9.
⊖ Colindale; Bus 79
10.00–18.00 Monday–Saturday; 14.00–18.00 Sunday;
Closed: Good Friday, 1st Monday May,
24, 25, 26 December, 1 January
A £, C £; Wheelchair/Shop/Food/Toilet

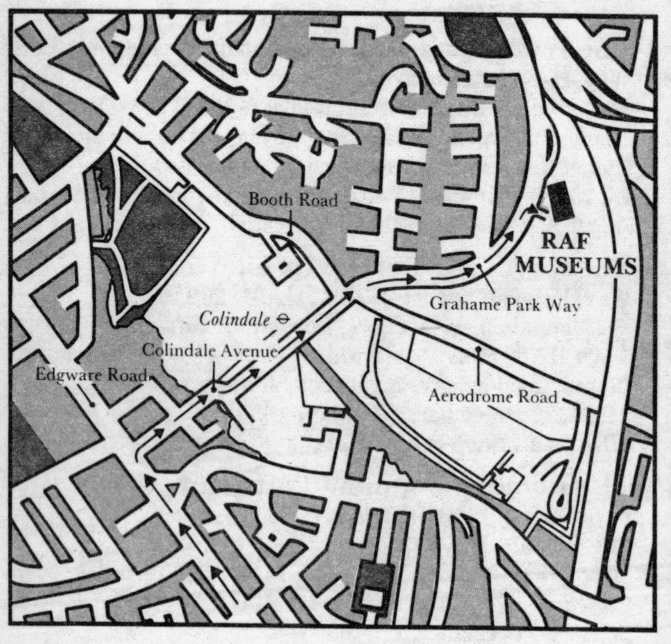

Booth Road
RAF MUSEUMS
Grahame Park Way
Colindale
Colindale Avenue
Edgware Road
Aerodrome Road

⊖ Colindale

When you come out of the Underground, turn left. It is some distance to the Museum, and it may be worth your while taking Bus 79 the rest of the way.

Bus 79
This bus goes down Colindale Avenue, but turns off before the Musems.

Car Go north on Edgware Road. Turn right into Colindale Avenue and carry on to a roundabout where the Museums are signposted.

There is a restaurant in the Battle of Britain Museum.

11.00 **The Battle of Britain Museum**

As you walk into the Museum you will see the wreck of a Hawker Hurricane which was shot down in 1940 while intercepting German aircraft.

Go into the room where you see the large white plane, passing an anti-aircraft gun which could fire to an altitude of 32,000 feet.

The white plane is a Short Sunderland, which patrolled the coasts looking for U-boats and carried depth-charges. Look at the underneath of the plane. It is shaped like a boat. The crew slept, cooked and lived for up to three weeks on this plane while at sea, only going on shore for repairs and stores.

Next is a Westland Lysander which was used for air-sea rescue. It also went to France in 1939 and worked there until the evacuation of Dunkirk. Note the window space which allowed the crew to have a wide area of vision outside.

The last plane is a Vickers Supermarine Seagull which was used during the Battle of Britain. It was also used for sea rescue and was catapulted from ships.

Now go up the stairs on your right. You are on a

level with the cockpit of the Sunderland. On one wall are photographs of a mixture of German Luftwaffe and RAF pilots. Walk to the opposite end, look down and you will see the Operation Room.

Go down the stairs at the opposite end to where you came up. Under the stairs is an Anderson Shelter and in it you will see a lady and her little girl.

In the same area, you will see a model of a London street during the Blitz, with examples of people who were involved in organizing rescue work and making sure that life continued as normally as possible.

There is a searchlight to illuminate enemy aircraft.

You will see a Women's Voluntary Service lady, a policeman, a scene of a radar operator and a WRAF (Women's Royal Air Force) folding a parachute.

Now start to walk round the perimeter of the hangar.

You will first see a fire-tender and an anti-aircraft gun with a photograph showing you a crew working a gun like this. There is a Gloster Gladiator, which intercepted the first bombing raids on Great Britain in Scotland in 1939. There is also a Boulton Paul Defiant which was used for night fighting.

If you go into the camouflaged building on the right you will see mementoes of the Battle of Britain.

When you come out, to your right you will see a Hawker Hurricane; there were more Hurricanes than any other planes in combat squadrons and they were in the thick of early air-fights over England and France. There is also a Heinkel HE 111, which was the Luftwaffe's best-known bomber plane.

Walking back down the hangar you will see a Junker JU 88D-1. This plane was flown to Aberdeen by a defecting German pilot. Notice the radar antenna. Nearby is a Messerschmitt, which was a night fighter; it also has a radar antenna on its nose.

Next is a small Italian Fiat, a plane used in the Spanish Civil War (1936–9). The Messerschmitt you next come to was hit while flying over the Thames. The pilot made a crash landing and was captured. The last plane is another Junker.

Now go out of the Museum and walk over towards the ship and into the Royal Air Force Museum.

13.00 **The Royal Air Force Museum**

Walk up the stairs and go into Gallery 1. Here you will see a glider made in 1910. It could be bought as a kit and was based on a design of the Wright Brothers.

You will walk through a gallery showing how thoughts of flight interested people hundreds of years ago. Leonardo de Vinci made many drawings of possible ways of flight, and in 1701 a Portuguese priest discovered the hot-air balloon.

You will see balloon baskets, Royal Engineers from 1878 and 1912, and a replica of an air ship 'envelope' (basket – look at the photo). You can see photos of early planes and pilots, models of various airfields, and a scene of a workshop with various engines in it.

In display cabinets are various trophies and mementoes of Lord Brabazon of Tara, especially a very old camera. There are also mementoes of other people, a larger workshop, and an old Crusley Tender. There is a scene of a radio operator with transmitter and a carrier pigeon. Look at the cockpits, the Women's Air Force display, various uniforms and ceremonial costumes. Then go into the gallery of people who won awards.

Now go out of the exit and downstairs.

At the beginning of this floor, you will see an armoured car, a desert air base, and the control cabin of a rigid airship. There is a Royal Observer Corps post, transmitters, guns, rifles, pilots in their sleeping quarters, and ejection seats.

Then have a look at the exhibition of the RAF as it

is today; there is a Nimrod cockpit. You will also see
a Vickers and a triplane with three wings, which
could climb very well and had good manoeuvrability;
it was very popular between 1917 and 1919.

The de Havilland Tiger Moth was a very aerobatic
plane, used for pilot training. There are Spitfires and
an early helicopter. There is also a Dornier, a German
sea-rescue plane with three engines. The only surviving Hawker Typhoon is here – a plane which had
many problems during the design stage and eventually was used to catch the low-flying Luftwaffe fighter
bombers. There is a Hawker Hunter interceptor
fighter and a Hawker P 1127. Notice the ejection
seats in the planes. The BAC Canberra was the first
jet to be used by the RAF.

14.00 The Bomber Command Museum

As you enter the Bomber Command Museum you will
see an Avro Lancaster. A bomb sits underneath it
with the bomb-bay open. Look at the side of the plane
by the cockpit and count how many bombing missions
it made. The Lancaster participated in every night
attack on Germany and is considered to be one of the
greatest planes in the history of aviation. These were
the planes that carried the Wallis skipping drum-
bomb used against dams.

There are many versions of the Vickers Wellington
bomber and it is thought to be an outstanding plane.

The Vickers Vimy was built in 1967 to commemorate the Atlantic crossing of 1919.

The large white plane, the Vickers Valiant, was
used until 1956. The Handly Page Halifax planes
were seven-seat bombers, and were also used as cargo
transport and paratroop carriers. This particular
plane was shot down over Norway and was recovered
in 1973. It is the only Halifax left.

The de Havilland Mosquito was designed in 1938 to

be an unarmed bomber. Twenty-nine versions of it
were made; the fighter-bomber, with a production of
2,584, was produced in greater quantities than any
other type.

The particular Avro Vulcan delta-wing you will see
started flying in 1961 and continued in service for 20
years.

Did You Know?

1. How many crew the anti-aircraft gun had?
2. How the spotlight found enemy aircraft?
3. If your grandparents had an Anderson shelter?
4. What the Women's Voluntary Service lady was doing?
5. When the first attack on England occurred in World War
   II?
6. Who rediscovered the balloon?
7. When the English Channel was first crossed by balloon?
8. What the man standing under a tree is doing?
9. What the pilot pulls to eject from the plane?

TOUR 24
The London Fashion Scene

1 King's Road, Chelsea, London SW3
 ⊖ Sloane Square; Bus 11, 19, 22, 137

2 Kensington Market, Kensington High St, London
W8
 ⊖ Kensington High St; Bus 9, 18, 31, 49, 73
10.00–17.30 Monday–Saturday. *Closed*: Sunday

3 Hyper-Hyper, 26–40 Kensington High St,
London W8
 ⊖ Kensington High St; Bus 9, 28, 31, 49, 73
10.00–18.00 Monday–Wednesday, Friday–Saturday
10.00–19.00 Thursday. *Closed*: Sunday

4 Carnaby Street
 ⊖ Oxford Circus or Piccadilly Circus

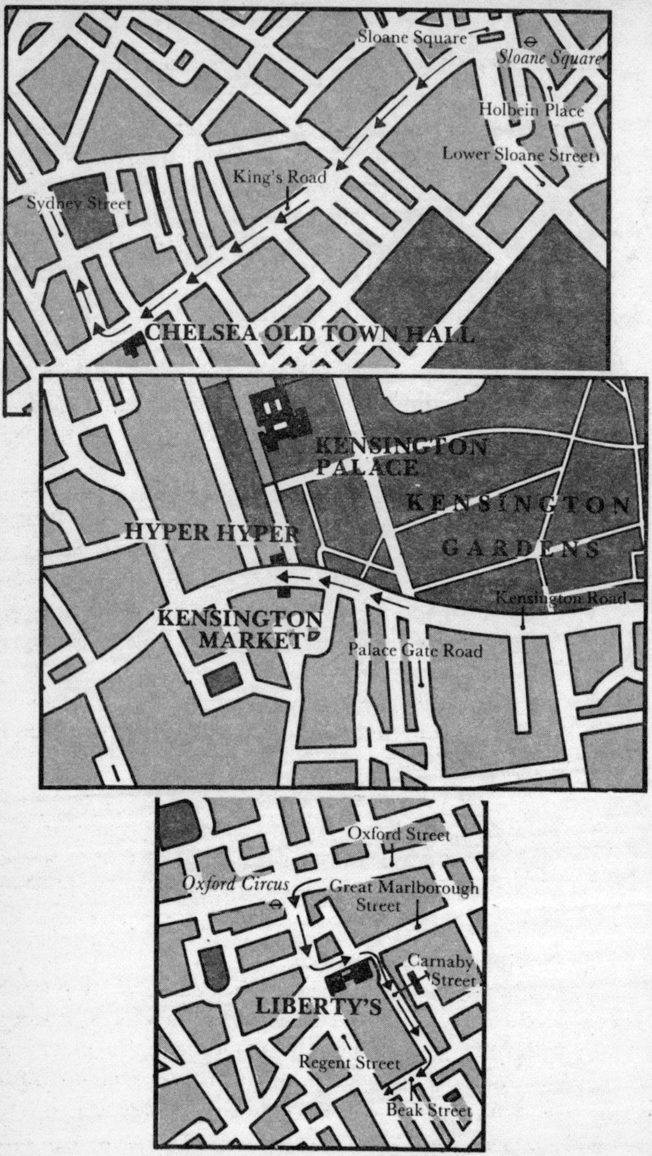

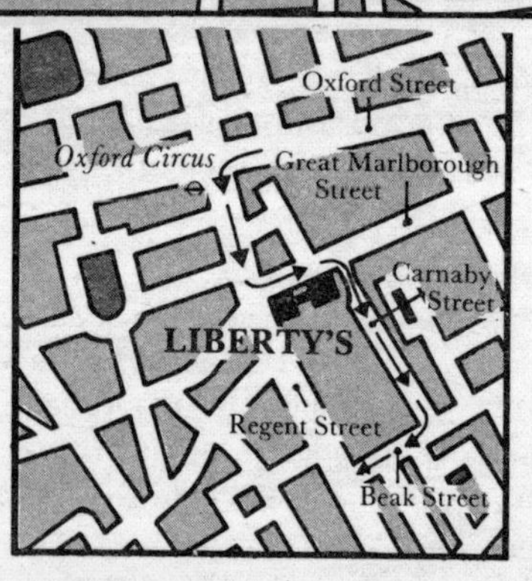

Sloane Square
Sloane Square
Holbein Place
Lower Sloane Street
King's Road
Sydney Street
CHELSEA OLD TOWN HALL
KENSINGTON PALACE
KENSINGTON GARDENS
HYPER HYPER
Kensington Road
KENSINGTON MARKET
Palace Gate Road
Oxford Street
Oxford Circus
Great Marlborough Street
Carnaby Street
LIBERTY'S
Regent Street
Beak Street

⊖ Sloane Square

This tour will be of special interest to teenagers wanting to shop for the latest English fashions.

Go out of the station and walk past Sloane Square, crossing to the right-hand side of King's Road, a haven for London's very colourful punks.

10.30 King's Road

You will go past many interesting shops selling a variety of clothing. Some of the shop displays are very interesting because of the mannequins (such as at Pashu Paris). Don't be afraid to pop in for a look — sales people are very friendly.

Cross the King's Road after the Markham Pub and go into the Great Gear Market where you will find punk styles, make-up, jewellery and records.

When you come out, continue in the same direction until you get to the Antique Market, an expensive but excellent market selling quality silver, jewellery, clocks, paintings, etc.

Continue down the King's Road until you get to the Old Town Hall and then cross and walk down Sidney Street to the bus stop.

Take a 49 bus to Kensington High Street. As you turn into it, you will see Kensington Palace across the street. Get off the bus outside Kensington Market.

12.00 Kensington Market

Kensington Market sells second-hand and new clothes, jewellery and shoes. There is a hairdresser, a tailor making suits on the premises, and a café. You can find Fifties and Sixties styles as well as punk clothing.

Leave the market to the right and cross the street. Go right until you come to Hyper-Hyper.

12.45 Hyper-Hyper

Hyper-Hyper began about two years ago as a means of helping young creative designers to find a market for their clothes. There is a fantastic range of designs and ideas with prices varying from £5 to £200. There are wigs, make-up, shoes, hats, bags and clothes.

Take a 73 bus when you leave Hyper-Hyper; this takes you to the top of Regent Street. Get off at the stop immediately after Regent Street.

Walk back in the direction from which you have just come. Cross Oxford Street and when you get to Regent Street, turn left. You will pass Laura Ashley, the famous chain of shops specializing in 'country' clothes, furnishings and accessories. Prices are considerably cheaper in the Laura Ashley shops in England than in other countries.

Turn left on Great Marlborough Street, cross over to the Liberty's side (Liberty's is worth a visit), and then turn right into Carnaby Street.

13.15 Carnaby Street

At Carnaby Street, you can find a mixture of different styles of clothes – punk, up-market and traditional.

Leave Carnaby Street and walk to Regent Street.

You can either walk back to Oxford Circus, which is on the Central, Bakerloo and Victoria Lines, or go to Piccadilly Circus, which has the Bakerloo and Piccadilly lines.

TOUR 25
Marx and the Market

1 **Waterlow Park,** Highgate Hill, London N6.
⊖ Archway then bus 143, 210 or 271 to Highgate
07.30–19.30 Daily

2 **Highgate Cemetery West,*** West Side, Swains
Lane, Highgate, London N6. Tel. (01) 340 1834
⊖ Archway then bus 143, 210 or 271 to Highgate
April–September: 10.00–16.00 Daily (*guided tours only*)
October–March: 10.00–15.00 (*guided tours only*)
Visitors' Special Days (no tours): 13.00–17.00
Shop

3 **Highgate Cemetery East,*** East Side, Swains
Lane, Highgate, London N6. Tel. (01) 340 1834
⊖ Archway then bus 143, 210 or 271 to Highgate
April–September: 09.00–16.00 Daily;
October–March: 09.00–17.00 Daily

4 **Camden Lock Market,** Chalk Farm Road,
London NW1.
⊖ Camden Town, Chalk Farm; Bus 3, 24, 27, 31, 53, 68,
134, 214
Only Saturday and Sunday

* Friends of Highgate Cemetery, 5 View Road, London N6. Tel.
(01) 348 0808 – for specialist groups with S.A.E.

Highgate High Street
WATERLOW PARK
Highgate Hill
HIGHGATE CEMETERY WEST SIDE
HIGHGATE CEMETERY EAST SIDE
Archway
Swain's Lane
Highgate Road
Haverstock Hill
Kentish Town Road
Chalk Farm
Chalk Farm Road
CAMDEN LOCK MARKET
Regent's Park Road
Camden Town
Bayham Road
Camden High Street
Regent's Canal
Parkway

⊖ Archway

10.00 If you arrive on a 271 bus, cross on the two pedestrian
       crossings which take you over South Grove. Walk
       down Highgate Hill.
          If you arrive on buses 143 or 210, get off on High-
       gate Hill at the stop just past the traffic lights. You
       will see the park with its trees.
          If you want to feed the squirrels, birds and ducks,
       be sure to bring food with you.
          If you would rather have a quiet, peaceful day, do
       this tour during the week and avoid Camden Lock
       Market. When you finish the cemeteries, just retrace
       your steps to Highgate.
          Try to arrive at Highgate Cemetery a bit before the
       hour so that you don't miss the guided tour.

In the Middle Ages, this area was covered by the
Forest of Middlesex and the Park of the Bishop of
London. Most of the houses and shops were built in
the 1700s.
   Walk down Highgate Hill and turn right into
Waterlow Park.

10.15 **Waterlow Park**
The park is named after Sir Sydney Waterlow, who
bought Lauderdale House in the 1800s. He gave the
park and house to the Borough of Camden and they
were opened to the public.
   Go on the left path. You can see tennis courts to
the right. You will come to a nature reserve; go left
and stay left until you reach a more formal garden,
then go left to Lauderdale House.
   Lauderdale House was built in the 1600s, but has
been rebuilt several times. There is a story that Nell
Gwynne once lived here and one day, when Charles II
was walking round the garden, she dangled her six-
year-old son out of the window and said that she

would drop him if he wasn't made a Duke immediately, which he was.

The house is now a community centre with classes for children and adults, art exhibitions and concerts. You can get a very good cup of coffee here and soft drinks for the children.

When you leave Lauderdale House, go down the steps to the side and then down the next set of steps. Keep walking left and you will find a few tropical birds in cages. Then go down the hill past the ponds. There are ducks to feed and squirrels are plentiful. Carry on curving right with the road.

Cross Swains Lane.

11.00 Highgate Cemetery West

The cemetery was opened in 1839 at a time when bodies were being snatched for medical dissection, metal from the coffins was being stolen, and bodies were being buried close to the surface and easily disturbed. Here, behind gates which could be locked and guarded at night, eternal rest in peace was assured for those people wealthy enough to be buried in this private sanctuary.

The cemetery was so popular that in 1859 more land was opened across Swains Lane. After the services in the chapel on this side, the coffins would be transported on cables across the road for burial. It was an expensive proposition to be buried here – the cost being roughly three times the average yearly wage.

A guide will take you around the cemetery. If you especially want to see the grave of someone, mention it to the guide. Make sure you see the Catacombs and the Egyptian Walk.

Some of the graves you can see belong to:
Charles Cruft (1852–1938), founder of the famous dog show.

Catherine Dickens, wife of Charles, and his parents.

Michael Faraday (1791–1867), discoverer of the elec-
tro-magnetic induction of electric currents.

John Galsworthy (1867–1933), novelist and playwright, who wrote *The Forsyte Saga*.

William Haseldine Pepys (d. 1856), founder of the
Geological Society.

The family of Gabrielle Rossetti (1783–1854), an Italian refugee, who became a Professor of Italian at
King's College, London.

Christina Georgina Rossetti (1830–94), a poet and
theological writer.

William Michael Rossetti (1829–1919), poet and
editor of a Pre-Raphaelite magazine.

Elizabeth Siddal (d. 1862), wife and model of son
Dante Gabriel Rossetti. He opened his wife's grave
to retrieve poems placed in it when she died.

Thomas Sayers (1826–65), the last bare-fisted boxer.

Anne Swanwick (1813–99), founder of Girton College,
Cambridge, and Somerville Hall, Oxford.

12.00 Highgate Cemetery East

After leaving the West side of Highgate Cemetery,
cross to the East side, where you will see the graves
of Karl Marx and George Eliot. Walk in through the
gate and carry on straight ahead. You will see Karl
Marx's very large grave ahead of you.

Karl Marx (1818–83) emigrated to London in 1849.
He collaborated with Friedrich Engels on the Commu-
nist Manifesto. Marx also wrote *Das Kapital*. He is
buried in the same grave as his daughter, Eleanor,
and her husband.

You will find the path to George Eliot's grave just a
bit before the grave of Karl Marx and to the left.

George Eliot (1819–80), whose real name was Mary
Ann Evans, was a novelist who wrote about provincial
life during the industrial revolution. She wrote

Middlemarch, Mill on the Floss and several other novels.

12.30   When you leave the Cemetery, walk down the hill on Swains Lane. On the right, you will see the Holly Lodge Estate, built between the wars in a mock Tudor style. The houses were built on the site of the house of Baroness Angela Burdett-Coutts, a close friend of Charles Dickens, who used much of her inheritance to build houses for the poor.

Further down the hill on your left, you will see Holly Village, Victorian Gothic cottages originally built by the Baroness for her retired servants and now privately owned.

You will pass a number of shops. Turn left at Highgate West Hill and rest while you wait for a bus to Camden Town. Or you could eat at the restaurant or snack bar across the street (not on Sundays).

Take a 214 bus to Camden Town. Get off the bus on Camden Road across from the Parish Church. Walk in the same direction as the bus is going. Cross at the pedestrian crossing. This is Bayham Street, where Charles Dickens lived when he moved to London at the age of 11.

Walk round and cross Greenland Road and Camden High Street. Turn right, cross Parkway, and then walk up Camden High Street, which eventually leads into Chalk Farm Road. On Saturdays and Sundays, this road is like one long market, with crowds of people shopping, browsing and searching for bargains.

You will pass a fruit and vegetable market on your left, and then Humla, a children's clothing shop specializing in bright-coloured Scandinavian knit-wear. On the right is Camden Market, mainly selling new and second-hand clothes.

Carry on, cross Camden Lock, which is on the Regent's Canal, and turn left. Have a look at the lock; you might well see longboats waiting for the level of the water to rise or sink. Then go into the Market.

13.00 Camden Lock Market

This market has become one of the most popular markets of North London. There are a great variety of stalls: ethnic clothes, Indian decorations, books, records, old clothes, craft items, antique furniture, old fireplaces, garden statues, clocks, handmade jumpers, rag rugs, lace curtains and tableclothes, pine and cane furniture, musical instruments, etc. There are stalls selling food and a very good French restaurant.

When you leave the market, you can either go left up Chalk Farm Road to Chalk Farm Underground, or you can go back the way you came to Camden Town Underground.

If you choose the first route, there are some lovely shops and interesting stalls on the opposite side of the road to Camden Lock Market. On the same side as the market, about 50 yards further, is another market with stalls both outside and inside a large building, mostly selling antiques and bric-à-brac.

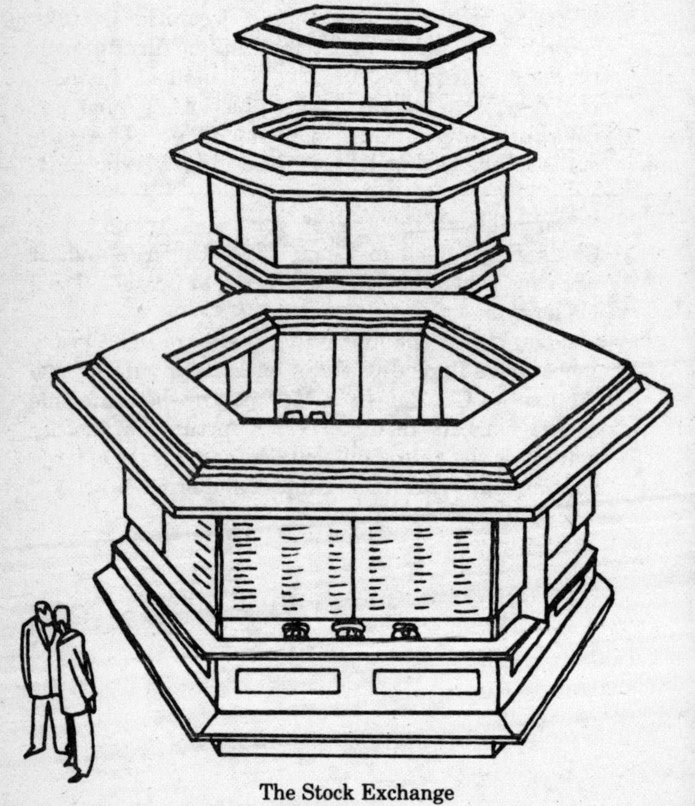

The Stock Exchange

TOUR 26
Money, Money, Money

1 The Stock Exchange, Old Broad Street, London
EC2
⊖ Bank, Monument; Bus 8, 15, 22, 25
Visitors' Gallery: 10.00–15.30 Monday–Friday;
Closed: Public Holidays, 24 December
There is a good children's book published on the Stock
Exchange.

2 The Royal Exchange, Cornhill and Threadneedle
Street, London EC2
⊖ Bank, Monument; Bus 8, 15, 22, 25
Visitors' Gallery: 11.30–13.00 Monday–Friday;
Closed: Public Holidays, 24 December

3 Guildhall, Gresham Street, London EC2 (P.O. Box
270, London EC2P 2EJ)
⊖ Bank, Moorgate, Mansion House, St Paul's; Bus 9, 11,
22, 76
10.00–17.00 Monday–Saturday; 10.00–17.00 Sunday
May–September, Spring and Autumn Bank Holidays;
Closed: Sunday October–April, Good Friday,
24, 25, 26 December, 1 January
For tours apply to City Guide, Public Relations Office.
Wheelchair/Toilet

4 The Clockmakers' Company Collection, The
Clock Room, Guildhall Library, Aldermanbury, London
EC2
⊖ Bank, Moorgate, Mansion House, St Paul's; Bus 9, 11,
22, 76
09.30–17.00 Monday–Friday; *Closed*: Saturday, Sunday,
Bank Holidays; Toilet

Note: The Lord Mayor's Show occurs on the second Saturday
in November. There is a procession with the Lord Mayor's
beautiful coach. Its route is from the Mansion House to the
Royal Courts of Justice on the Strand.

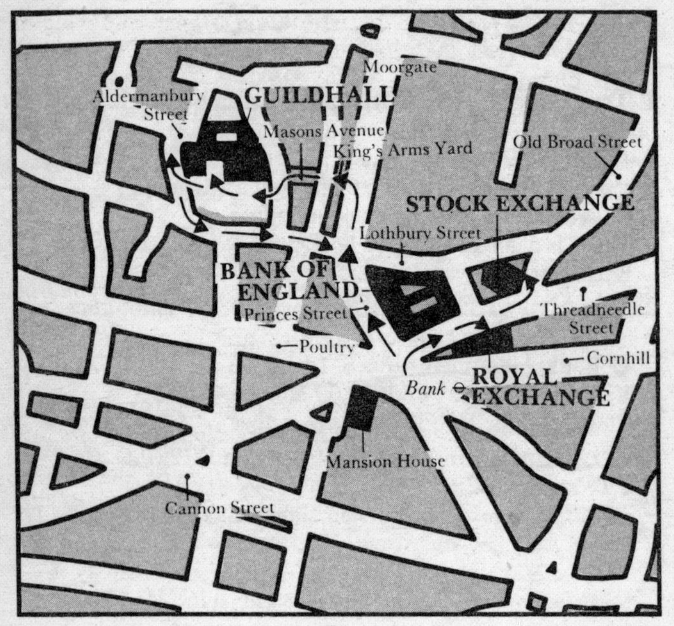

Moorgate
Aldermanbury Street
GUILDHALL
Masons Avenue
King's Arms Yard
Old Broad Street
STOCK EXCHANGE
Lothbury Street
BANK OF ENGLAND
Princes Street
Threadneedle Street
Poultry
Cornhill
Bank
ROYAL EXCHANGE
Mansion House
Cannon Street

⊖ Bank

The Bank Underground Station is very confusing as it services Northern, Central, Circle and District lines.

Whatever line you arrive on, exit where it is marked 'Baltic Exchange, Cornhill, Lloyds, Royal Exchange, Stock Exchange, Threadneedle Street'.

10.30 When you arrive at the top of the stairs, stand in the open area and have a look round. Face the statue of a man on horseback. Mansion House is in front and slightly to the left of the statue.

The **Mansion House** was designed by George Dance the Elder (1700–1768) in the mid-1700s and is now the official residence of the Lord Mayor of London. Before the building of Mansion House, the Mayors lived in their own homes.

To the right is the **Bank of England**. Notice how small the door is in this huge building. The Bank was built just before World War II.

Behind you is the **Royal Exchange**.

Walk down Threadneedle Street and cross at the pedestrian crossing. Continue walking in the same direction, veering to the left into Old Broad Street. The Stock Exchange will be on your left.

10.45 The Stock Exchange

When you go in, ask for the Visitors' Gallery, which is up some stairs.

This Gallery allows you to view the floor of the Stock Exchange; it looks very confusing to anyone who isn't knowledgeable about it. There are maps of the Exchange floor to explain where certain kinds of stocks are dealt with. There is also a map of the world on the wall facing you with clocks showing times for different places in the world.

The people sitting at the octagonal sites are called 'jobbers' and they buy and sell shares. Where they stand is called a 'pitch'. Stockbrokers representing people wanting to invest their money approach 'jobbers' and determine a price for buying or selling a particular share.

Every half-hour or so you can listen to a commentary about what you are looking at and see a 20-minute film.

11.30 When you leave the Stock Exchange, return the way you came, but after crossing Threadneedle Street, turn left. You will see a small area with benches. There are two sandwich shops nearby in which to buy some lunch.

While you are here, look up at the Tower of the Royal Exchange. There is a statue of Sir Thomas Gresham (1519–79), who built the first Royal Exchange at his own expense. Notice his family crest above him on the weather-vane.

Now walk round to the front of the Royal Exchange and go in.

12.00 **The Royal Exchange**

Try to arrive here at 12.00 as a carillon (bells played by a person using a type of organ) plays English, Scots, Welsh, Irish, Canadian and Australian melodies (not all at once). At Christmas-time, carols are played.

Normal dealing in stocks and shares moved to the Stock Exchange in 1982. The Royal Exchange (named by Queen Elizabeth I) is now occupied by The London International Financial Futures Exchange (LIFFE).

Go up to the Visitors' Gallery to the right.

The scene is much like the one at the Stock Exchange, but on a smaller scale. The people wearing powder-blue coats are LIFFE staff. They sit in pulpits and monitor trade. The people wearing mustard-yellow coats are training to be members. They do the paper work and act as messengers. The red jackets are provided by LIFFE for people who work for companies who buy and sell here; some companies provide their own jackets.

12.30 When you leave the Royal Exchange, walk to the statue and cross to the Bank of England side of Threadneedle Street. Turn into Princes Street. Go through the arch and cross Lothbury Street and then left across Moorgate Street.

Walk up Moorgate Street, turn left into Great Bell Alley, cross Coleman Street to the bollards and go straight on, passing a pub called Old Dr Butler's Head. You can see part of the Guildhall in front of you at the end of the passage. Cross the street.

Turn left and then turn right at a passage called Guildhall Buildings, passing the Mayor's and City of London Court, to the yard of Guildhall. Go into the modern entrance on the right.

13.00 Guildhall

The first Mayor was installed in this Guildhall in 1192, but Richard Whittington (c. 1363–1423) is the most famous Lord Mayor of London. He was Mayor four times, in 1397, 1397–8, 1406–7 and 1419–20. Some of the walls in the Guildhall date from 1400.

Walk straight ahead. The entrance to the Great Hall is to your right. Walk around to your left. There are various statues around the perimeter of the hall – there is one to the memory of Horatio Nelson (1758–1805), and one of the Duke of Wellington (1769–1852). William Pitt the Elder (1708–78) and William Pitt the Younger (1759–1806) are there. There is a list of trials held in Guildhall. As you walk back, you will see Gog and Magog on either sides of the hall – they are figures from old pageants played at midsummer. Notice the banners of the Livery Companies around the hall and the measures along the left.

As you walk back to the entrance, turn right and you will see gifts in cases. There is the sculptured head of a Prince and at the end of the passage a clock with a blacksmith hammering metal; he is beating the minutes.

Walk back to the entrance.

When you leave, go to the right and through the archway. Then turn right and walk until you see the entrance to the Library on your right. As you enter the Clock Museum is on your left.

13.30 Clockmakers' Company Collection

In the first case you will see small clocks and watches available when the Clockmakers' Company was founded in 1631. There is an astrolabe (used to calculate the distance of stars) and a pocket sundial.

The long cases have watches grouped according to age. There are Verge watches of 1600–1660, 1660–1710 and the 18th Century. There is a case of Marine Chronometers, which were used for measuring time on ships before radios were invented. You will also see a prototype of the first temperature compensation device in a clock.

The long cases continue with Verge watches of the 18th Century, 18th–19 Centuries, and then move on to cylinder watches of 1700–1900. Next are duplex watches of 1789–1910, detente watches of 1775–1815 and to 1883; and lever watches of 1785–1928.

Then there are long-case clocks, tavern clocks, table clocks, skeleton clocks, a rolling ball clock and a gas-operated clock. There is also a very interesting collection of watch keys.

In the Library Shop (which is two floors up), you can buy very nice map prints and prints of old paintings or engravings.

When you leave the Library, turn left and walk to Gresham Street. Turn left. Cross Moorgate and turn right, crossing Lothbury. Walk back along the side of the Bank of England and cross Threadneedle Street to the Royal Exchange and down to the Underground.

Did You Spot?

1. The man on horseback? What is his name?
2. What is on top the weathervane?
3. The man sitting in the armchair? Who is it?
4. The prince's head? Which prince is it?

Do You Know?

5. What animal is connected with Dick Whittington?
6. The name of the lady who was Queen of England for nine days?
7. The lengths of the measures?
8. When the astrolabe was made?
9. Who the skull watch belonged to?
10. What kind of clock has sand in it?

TOUR 27
Justice and Dr Johnson

1 The Central Criminal Court, Old Bailey,
London EC4. Tel. (01) 348 3277
St. Paul's; Bus 8, 22, 25
When in Session: 10.15–13.00, 13.50–16.00
Monday–Friday
Closed: Saturday, Sunday, Bank Holidays, Good Friday,
24, 25, 26 December, 1 January
No one admitted under 14 years of age. Those aged 14–17
must be accompanied by an adult. No tape recorders or
cameras allowed; Toilet

2 Dr Johnson's House, 17 Gough Square, London
EC4. Tel. (01) 353 3745
Chancery Lane, Temple; Bus 4, 5, 8, 9, 11, 15, 18, 22,
23, 25, 45, 46, 63, 141
October–April: 11.00–17.00 Monday–Saturday;
May–September: 11.00–17.30 Monday–Saturday. *Closed*:
Sunday, Bank Holiday, Good Friday, 24 December
A £, C £, P £, S £

3 The Royal Courts of Justice, Strand, London
WC2. Tel. (01) 405 7641
Temple, Holborn, Chancery Lane; Bus 171
10.30–16.30 Monday–Friday. *Closed*: Saturday and Sunday
Wheelchair/Shop/Food/Toilet
No one admitted under 14 years of age. Those aged 14–17
must be accompanied by an adult. No tape recorders or
cameras allowed.

4 The Temple, 16–17 Fleet Street, London EC4
Temple; Bus 171
Inner Temple Gateway: 08.00–20.00 Monday–Friday
Middle Temple Hall: 10.00–12.00, 15.00–16.30
Monday–Friday *Closed*: Saturday and Sunday

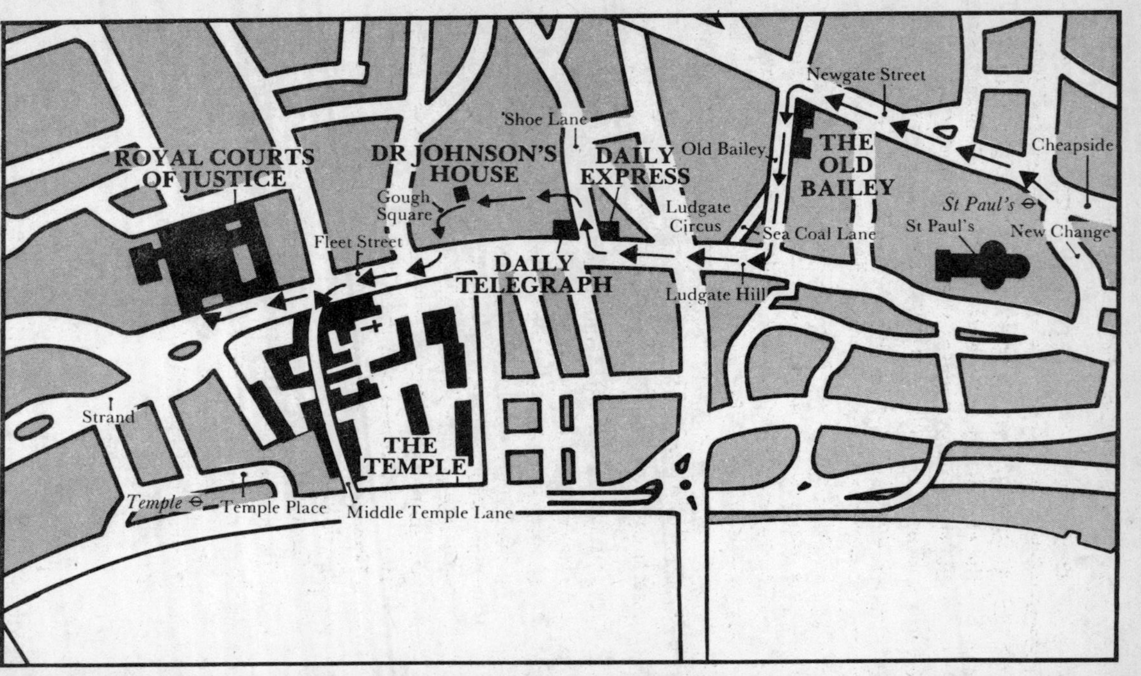

Cheapside
New Change
St Paul's
St Paul's
Newgate Street
THE OLD BAILEY
Sea Coal Lane
Old Bailey
DAILY EXPRESS
Ludgate Circus
Ludgate Hill
Shoe Lane
DR JOHNSON'S HOUSE
DAILY TELEGRAPH
Gough Square
Fleet Street
THE TEMPLE
Middle Temple Lane
ROYAL COURTS OF JUSTICE
Temple Place
Temple
Strand

⊖ St Paul's

11.15 At St Paul's, go out of the exit to the right leading to the Old Bailey. At street level, Cheapside Street is to the right and Newgate Street to the left. Go left.

The large old buildings across the street are a National Postal Museum, St Bartholomew's Hospital, better known as Barts Hospital, and Christ Church. Cross Warwick Lane. A little further on, you will see a large wooden gate. The next door is one of the entrances to the Visitors' Galleries of the Old Bailey. Push the button.

11.30 The Old Bailey

The Old Bailey began life as the Newgate Prison, built in the 1700s on the site of an earlier medieval prison. As the name implies, it was near the New Gate, and built on common land outside the walls of the City of London. There was another medieval prison next to the River Fleet. Because Newgate prison was such an unsavoury place, the judges carried nosegays to avoid catching gaol fever, and they still do so to this day. The present court was built in 1907. As you will see, there is a large concentration of law practices and courts in the area where you will be walking.

Go up the stairs and through the door at the top left. You will see Galleries 2, 3, and 4. A guard will be on duty who will tell you what trials there are in the courts. It is very important that you are quiet while you are in the gallery and when you go in and out.

The person being accused of a crime is called a defendant (defend). The person who has been damaged is called the plaintiff (from complaint). The Usher swears the witness in with an oath. Each person eligible to vote (on the Voting Register) is liable to be called for Jury Service. Barristers (called to the Bar) represent the plaintiff and defendant. Solicitors formerly solicited clients for the barristers and now provide the information the barrister needs to plead the case. Notice that the barristers, Clerk and Judge are wearing wigs. This practice of wearing wigs has carried on since the 18th Century when wigs were very popular.

Leave the Old Bailey the way you came in. As you come down the steps, notice the door for the prisoners' visitors.

Go left on Old Bailey Street past the new part of the Old Bailey. On your left, you will see, behind a glass door, listings of all the trials taking place and how they have progressed.

You will see several places to eat as you walk along. When you arrive at Ludgate Hill, turn right, cross Old Bailey Street and walk towards the bridge. Cross Sea Coal Lane and Ludgate Circus, continuing straight ahead. As you walk along, you will see something on a bar above your head.

You will pass the offices of the *Daily Express* newspaper. Turn right into Shoe Lane where you will go past the *Daily Telegraph*. Turn left at the bollards and walk along the back of the *Daily Telegraph* building. If it is a warm day, the doors may be open so that you can see the printing presses. Go under the arch. You will see the London Broadcasting Corporation (LBC) radio offices. At the top of the square is Dr Johnson's House.

13.00 **Dr Johnson's House**

Dr Johnson (1709–84) moved into this house in 1748 to be close to the printer of his dictionary, whose printing presses were in the next square to the north. He lived here until 1759; his wife died while living here.

His dictionary was finished in 1755 and went through four printings while he was alive. It was published for 100 years until eventually replaced by the *Oxford Dictionary*. In the house you will see an example of a dictionary in use at the time and a page of his own dictionary. The word given as an example is 'heart'.

Although he received £1,575 to cover the costs of writing the dictionary and a few other smaller payments, he had to employ six people to compile the words to be used, and was always running short of money. He was actually under arrest in 1756 for a debt of 'Five Pounds, Eighteen Shillings'. In 1762, he was finally given a pension of £300 a year by George III (1738–1820).

Dr Johnson met James Boswell (1740–95) at a house in Covent Garden in 1763. It is only through the diary of James Boswell that we know very much about Dr Johnson.

You will see paintings of many famous people who visited Dr Johnson at this house, such as the Methodist preacher John Wesley (1703–91), the painter Sir Joshua Reynolds (1723–92), the actor David Garrick (1717–79), the actor and playwright Richard Sheridan (1751–92), the actress Mrs Sarah Siddons (1755–1831), and the author Fanny Burney (1752–1840). Because Dr Johnson was a wonderful conversationalist his company was much sought after. There is also a portrait of Francis Barber, his servant.

When you come out of the house, you will see a passage leading off the square. Walk down it to Fleet

Street. Turn right and walk to the Royal Courts of Justice, which will be on your right.

14.30 The Royal Courts of Justice

These courts deal with civil justice – the relationships and disputes that arise between private individuals. They are not like courts such as the Old Bailey, which have to do with cases involving the individual and the State. The Court of Appeals is also here, dealing with both civil and criminal appeals.

The Courts were built in 1874–82 to replace the destroyed courts round Westminster Hall. As you walk in, you will see the Great Hall with the courts off to the side and on the upper floors. You can visit most courts, although some will be closed to visitors. There is no one to direct you to a particular court.

Notice the long, dark halls, hidden flights of curved steps, and tight groups of barristers discussing their cases.

When you come out, cross Fleet Street (or the Strand) and go left. Walk until you come to the passage to the Inner Temple and then turn right.

15.00 The Temple

The Inns of Court – Lincoln's Inn (1310), Middle Temple (1340), Inner Temple (1340) and Gray's Inn (1357) – take in students to study law and are able to confer the degree of Barrister-at-Law. The barrister's offices are called 'chambers'.

Walk straight ahead; you will see a sign indicating The Temple Church. The entrance is on the south side and you will see the porch as you curve round.

The Temple Church

This Church was built by the Knights Templar (founded c. 1120) as the chapel to their monastery.

They aided poor pilgrims on their voyages to the Holy Land. Inside you can see effigies of knights.

When you come out, go through the Arches and veer left. Go down the steps and then straight through the arch. Cross Middle Temple Lane and go up the steps and into Middle Temple Hall.

Middle Temple Hall

This Elizabeth Great Hall is very famous for its double hammer-beam ceiling and wood-panelled walls, and also because there is a tradition that Queen Elizabeth I (1533–1603) saw the first performance of *Twelfth Night* by William Shakespeare (1564–1616) here in 1602. You can see portraits of Charles I (1600–1649), Charles II (1633–85) and Queen Elizabeth I.

When you leave Middle Temple Hall, turn right into Middle Temple Lane. Walk to the end and turn right, walking until you reach Temple Place. Curve right with the road round the park, and on the other side you will find Temple Underground.

Did You Spot?
1. What was near the policeman guarding the defendant(s)?
2. How many jurors there were?
3. What was missing on the door?
4. What was on the bar over the street?
5. What Dr Johnson's wife was called?
6. How Samuel Johnson abbreviated Samuel?

Do You Know?
7. How the old dictionary defined 'heart'?
8. What the old chair in the parlour is called?
9. What Johnson insisted on before he employed Francis Barber?
10. In what part of the house Johnson wrote his dictionary?

TOUR 28
Everything but Petticoats

1 **Petticoat Lane Market,** Middlesex St, London EC3
⊖ Broad Street, Liverpool St; Bus 9, 11, 149 (from
Liverpool St end), 5, 10, 15, 23, 25, 40, 42, 67, 78, 253
(from Aldgate end)
Sunday: 10.00–14.00; *Closed*: Monday–Saturday

2 **The Hoop and Grapes Pub,** 47 Aldgate High St,
London EC3. Tel. (01) 480 5739
⊖ Aldgate; Bus 5, 10, 15, 23, 25, 40, 42, 67, 78, 253
11.30–15.00 and 17.00–20.30 Monday–Friday;
12.00–14.00 Sunday *Closed*: Saturday
No children under 14 allowed. No garden.
Food/Toilet

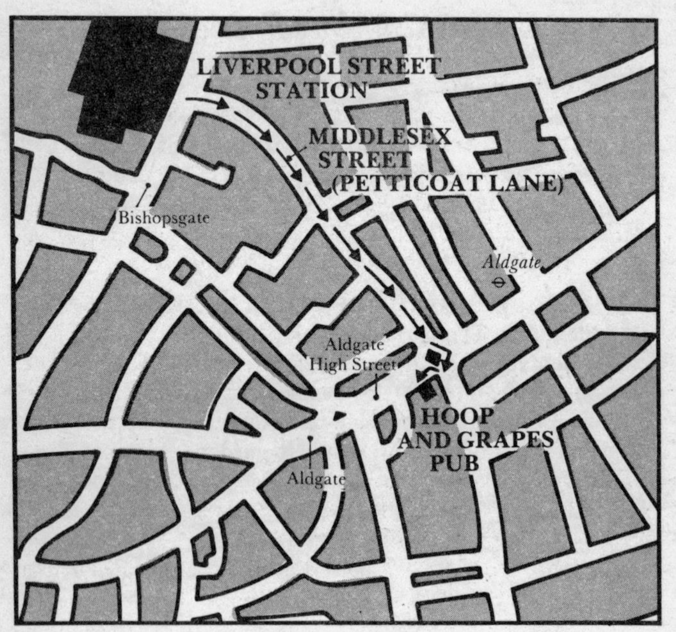

LIVERPOOL STREET STATION
MIDDLESEX STREET (PETTICOAT LANE)
Bishopsgate
Aldgate
Aldgate High Street
Aldgate
HOOP AND GRAPES PUB

⊖ Liverpool Street

The market can be very crowded and young children might well find it disturbing to be hemmed in by crowds of people. If you take young children, keep a good eye on them as they could easily get lost.

11.30 When you arrive at Liverpool St Underground, go out of the exit to Bishopsgate. Go up the stairs at the end of the passage, turn right, and go up more stairs and out onto the street.

Liverpool St Station stands on the site of the medieval monastery of St Mary-at-Bethlehem, founded in 1247. By 1377, it had become a lunatic asylum, the name of Bedlam being a corruption of Bethlehem.

If you look at a map, it is easy to see where the old London Wall ran – along the street called London Wall – starting at the Barbican, running across Moorgate, across Bishopsgate, and down the western side of Houndsditch to Aldgate. As Moorgate, Bishopsgate and Aldgate imply, these were gates through the walls leading into the old City of London. Bishopsgate Street has been a main road to East Anglia since the Roman occupation. Houndsditch Street was in fact a ditch where rubbish, including dead dogs, was dumped – hence the name.

Cross Bishopsgate and turn left. Turn right down Middlesex Street. Petticoat Lane Market begins a little way down the street.

11.45 **Petticoat Lane Market**
There is a jumble of clothes, jewellery, electrical equipment, tools, shoes, tableware, watches, suitcases and, perhaps, parrots to have your photo taken with. You can sample cockles, herrings, winkles, whelks, mussels and prawns. There are the traditional market

traders who fast-talk and juggle breakable objects. Beware of perfumed water.

When you get to the end of Middlesex Street, cross to the other side of Aldgate. There you will see the Hoop and Grapes Pub.

12.45 Hoop and Grapes Pub

The Hoop and Grapes has only been a pub for the last 100 years or so. It was built before 1666 and is the only timber-frame house left in the city of London. It has been a butcher's and a vintner's (wine seller) shop.

It is said that it was a stopping place for people walking their cattle from the country into Smithfield Market.

You can either walk back to Liverpool Street, or go to Aldgate Underground Station. There is a bus station just next to the Hoop and Grapes.

TOUR 29
Who'll Buy My Oranges?

1 Covent Garden Market, Covent Garden,
London WC2
⊖ Covent Garden

2 The Transport Museum, 39 Wellington Street,
London WC2. Tel. (01) 379 6344
⊖ Covent Garden
10.00–18.00 every day; *Closed*: 25, 26 December
A ££, C £, S £, Family £££; Wheelchair/Shop/Toilet

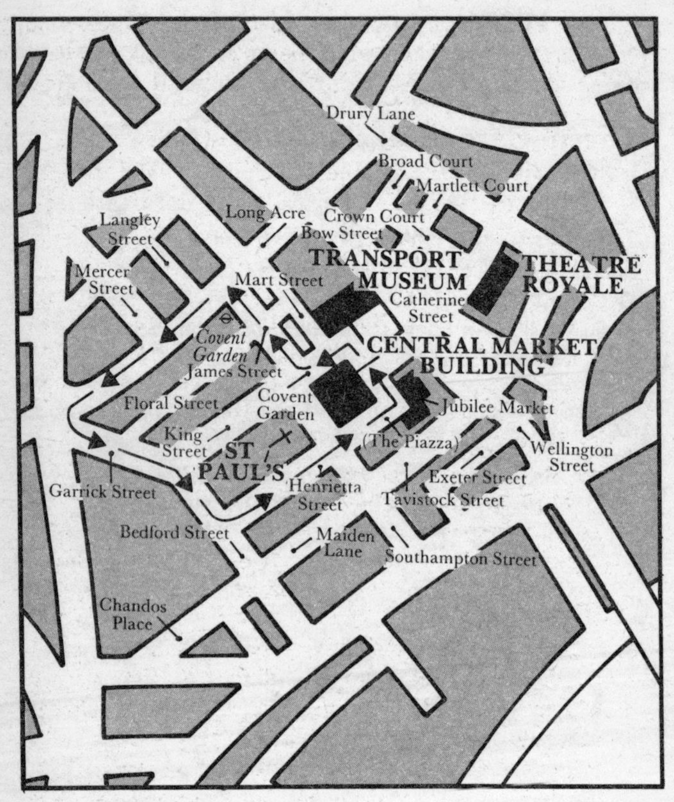

Drury Lane
Broad Court
Martlett Court
Crown Court
Langley
Street
Long Acre
Bow Street
TRANSPORT
MUSEUM
THEATRE
ROYALE
Mercer
Street
Mart Street
Catherine
Street
Covent
Garden
CENTRAL MARKET
BUILDING
James Street
Covent
Garden
Jubilee Market
Floral Street
King
Street
Wellington
Street
ST
PAUL'S
(The Piazza)
Garrick Street
Henrietta
Street
Exeter Street
Tavistock Street
Bedford Street
Maiden
Lane
Southampton Street
Chandos
Place

⊖ Covent Garden

Covent Garden's name comes from the Benedictine Convent of St Peter, which had a market garden here in the Middle Ages. Their land extended up to Long Acre.

At the time of the dissolution of the Monasteries in the early 1500s, the land was given to John Russell, the first Earl of Bedford. In 1613, the third Earl put a brick wall around an area of about 20 acres and the fourth Earl developed the area. It is considered to be the first major piece of town planning in London.

King, Henrietta, Russell and James Streets all led into the centre of the development, the Piazza and the Church. It was developed as residential accommodation for 'gentlemen', and the Piazza was designed to be an open space for exercise and social meetings. By the 1700s, there was a thriving market selling fresh produce to Londoners and a large number of coachmakers with supporting craftsmen of lamps, upholstery, trimmings, etc. There were also a large number of inns and coffee-houses for people attending the theatre.

Many famous people have associations with Covent Garden, including Henry Fielding (1707–54), author of *The History of Tom Jones*, who lived on Bow Street and held court there as a Justice of the Peace; he also organized the 'Bow Street Runners', who were pre-'Peelers', or early policemen. Nell Gwynne (1650–87) acted at the Drury Lane Theatre. The Civil Service Store on Chandos Place is the site of the blacking factory where Charles Dickens (1812–70) worked; Dickens's office for *Household Words* was at 26 Wellington Street. The first Sainsbury shop was opened in Drury Lane in 1869. Samuel Johnson (1709–84) lodged in Exeter Street when he first arrived in London. The artist J.M.W. Turner (1775–1851) was baptized in the Church and was born in Maiden Lane. King Edward VII (1841–1910) entertained Lily Langtry, the actress, at Rules Restaurant in Maiden Lane.

11.00 You will come out of the underground on James Street. Walk left to Long Acre and cross.

Go into the General Store, an old-fashioned shop full of oriental things. You will see a beautiful array of basket-work, rugs, wind chimes and mobiles. There are also practical jokes, small toys for children, glassware and pottery.

When you come out, go right down Long Acre. No. 30–31 on the left was built in 1870 for a firm of coachmakers. The street was known for its coachmakers in the 18th Century, and at one time there were 35 firms here. Samuel Pepys (1633–1703) mentioned that he came to Long Acre to buy a coach.

On the left you will also see Stamford Maps. The building only dates from the early 1900s, but the business has been there since 1880.

Cross the street and go down Garrick Street. This street is named after the actor David Garrick (1717–79). Across the street is the Garrick Club, opened in 1864; it used to be around the corner in King Street. It was there, in 1858, that Charles Dickens and William Makepeace Thackeray (1811–63) had their famous argument about an article written by a journalist named Edmund Yates about Thackeray. Dickens and Thackeray subsequently didn't speak to each other for five years.

Cross King Street and turn down Bedford Street. On the left side is a handsome red-brick building of 1873 which houses Macmillan, the publishers. Further down the road on the left is where *The Lady* magazine has been published since 1885.

Turn left into Henrietta Street. On the right side,

you will see houses 9–10, built in 1726–7. Jane Austen's (1775–1817) brother was a partner in the banking firm of Austen, Maude & Tilson at No. 10 during the years 1807–16. She stayed there while visiting London twice in the early 1800s.

No. 11 is where Charles Dickens's publishers, Chapman & Hall, had their premises from the 1800s to World War II.

Cross the cobbled area near Covent Garden Market at an angle and go right down the side of the Market Hall. You will pass Pollock's Toy Theatre to the left. At the end, to the right, is the Transport Museum.

12.00 The Transport Museum

In the shop you can buy a log card to use when you go in to clock how long you spend in the museum.

As you go in you will see a 1928 poster on the value of using the Underground. You will see engravings of various types of transport and then see models. There is a short-stage coach, a cabriolet (from which the word cab comes), an omnibus, a Hansom cab, horse-pulled and electric trams, and finally motorized buses.

Now move into the area of the full-sized buses and trams, walking up and down between them. There are buses similar to today's, old trams and old horse-drawn buses. You can get into the driver's seat of a modern bus.

After walking up a wooden ramp, you will find electric trams and wooden rail carriages. You will see an explanation of how tunnels are made for the Underground trains, and see the equipment needed to run the trains.

Go down the steps. You will see a model of the Bank Underground Station. Go into the next room and up the stairs. Here is a model of the Metropolitan railway, a full-sized Metropolitan Railway electric locomotive and a tube stock-car.

Go back to the entrance.

13.00 There are many places around or in Covent Garden where you can eat lunch. Wander around the market, look in the shops and go to the Jubilee Market, which is supposed to be one of the least expensive in London. In the Market Hall you will find stalls full of artisan goods, hand-made jumpers, toys, jewellery, pottery, etc. On most days you will be able to see performers: jugglers, dancers, jazz groups, singers, break-dancing, or mime. Covent Garden Market changes its character from day to day.

When you want to leave, head towards the Transport Museum. Go up James Street, which leads off the Market. The entrance to Covent Garden Underground is just around the corner on Long Acre.

Did You Spot?
1. How many people were on the garden seat omnibus?
2. What the drivers of the horse-drawn coaches used to get the horses to move?
3. What was different about the headlights of the wartime bus?

Do You Know?
4. Why there is mesh on the windows of the wartime bus?
5 Why one carriage was called the 'padded cell'?

TOUR 30

And the Animals Went in Two by Two

1 Little Venice to the Zoo on Regent's Canal,
London Waterbus Company, Camden Lock, London NW1.
Tel (01) 482 2550
⊖ Camden Town or Chalk Farm; Bus Little Venice 6, 8,
16, 16A, 176; Camden Town 24, 27, 28, 31, 68, 74, 134,
214, 718
Combined ticket for waterbus and zoo (one-way):
From Camden Lock: A £££, C ££; From Little Venice,
A £££, C ££ (On weekends only during winter)

2 London Zoo, Regent's Park, London NW1.
Tel. (01) 722 3333
⊖ Camden Town; Bus 3, 53, 74
Summer: 09.00–18.00 Monday–Saturday;
09.00–19.00 Sunday and Bank Holidays
Winter: 10.00– dusk daily
Closed: Christmas Day
A £££, C ££ 5–16, under 5 free, P ££, S ££
Wheelchair/Toilet/Shop/Food

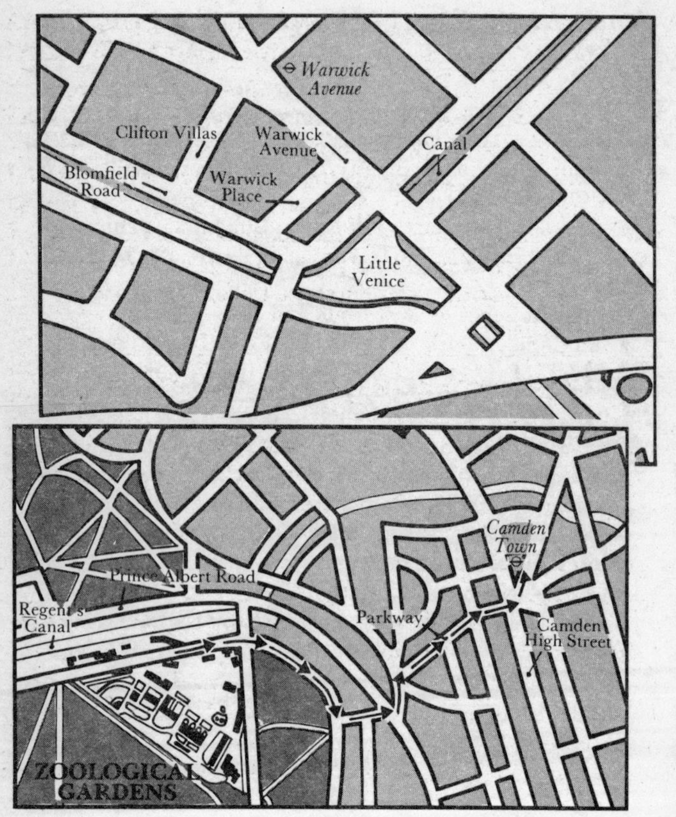

Warwick Avenue
Clifton Villas
Warwick Avenue
Canal
Blomfield Road
Warwick Place
Little Venice
Prince Albert Road
Camden Town
Regent's Canal
Parkway
Camden High Street
ZOOLOGICAL GARDENS

● Warwick Avenue

You can get to the Zoo by way of the Regent's Canal, a most enjoyable ride from Little Venice to the Zoo.

10.45　When you arrive at Warwick Avenue Underground, cross Warwick Avenue and go straight down Clifton Villas. At the end, turn left into Blomfield Road, which runs alongside the Canal, and walk to the bridge. Cross it and go down to the side of the canal. There is an area for the longboats to moor and a bench to sit on while you wait. The waterbuses run every hour and you purchase tickets once you are on the boat.

11.00　Little Venice to the Zoo on Regent's Canal

The first part of Regent's Canal was opened in 1816. What had been Marylebone Park was renamed Regent's Park, after the Prince Regent (George IV, 1762–1820). The architect John Nash (1752–1835) developed the area, and you will see some of his houses alongside the canal.

Little Venice, where you board the waterbus, is also called Browning's Pool, as Robert Browning, the poet (1812–89), once lived nearby. There are houseboats, pleasure boats and an art gallery, moored here.

You will pass through several tunnels. Remember than when horses pulled boats like these, they couldn't do the pulling when the boats went through long tunnels. The people on the boats had to lie on their backs and use their feet against the walls to push the boats through.

As you arrive in Regent's Park, you will see Lord Snowdon's Aviary and some antelope and deer on your right.

11.30 **London Zoo**

Feeding times:
    Sea Lions   15.00 Not Fridays;   14.30 October–March
    Penguins   14.30
    Reptiles   14.30 Fridays only
    Pelicans   14.45
    Animal rides 13.45 to 16.45, Easter to October
    Elephant weighing and Meet the Animals Show in
    the afternoon, Easter to October

The Zoological Society of London was founded in 1826 by a group of men including Sir Stamford Raffles, the founder of the colony of Singapore. When the Gardens first opened to the public in 1827, they were much smaller than today. The animals housed in the Lion Tower at the Tower of London were moved here in 1834 because they were too crowded. As this was a great time for exploration and the public was very enthusiastic to see such a variety of animals, the Zoo received animals from all over the world.

Don't forget that the Zoo's prime reason for existence is for zoological research, which helps in breeding animals and conserving them in the wild.

The Zoo has recently installed ten red squirrels in Regent's Park. They are being monitored with radio tags and specially designed feeding boxes have been made for them which are inaccessible to the larger grey squirrel. The Zoo would like people to tell them when and where they see red squirrels, so that they can determine by how much the population increases.

It is important that you do not feed the animals. Monkeys are extremely susceptible to human viruses, so that if you give them a left-over bit of sandwich, you might be transmitting a virus which could kill them.

Do not lean too far over the cages, as some of

the animals are light-fingered and can easily snatch something you are carrying.

In one year, the elephants lifted 14 coats, 12 handbags, 10 cameras, eight gloves and six return tickets to Leicester!

Once you enter the Zoo, go over the bridge. You will see sacred ibis, herons, African cattle egrets, and Mandarin ducks. The owls and pheasants are back along the way you came, past the bridge.

Now recross the bridge, go through the tunnel, and you will arrive at the front entrance to the Zoo.

Near the entrance you will find monkeys, apes and pandas. If you are lucky, you may see some babies nestling up to their mothers or swinging unsteadily from branch to branch. You will see the finely decorated face of the male mandrill and the male gorilla named Kumba.

To the left is a covered picnic area with tables. You will also find a restaurant and cafeteria, a bar and another café.

After eating, go to the bird section which includes water fowl and birds of prey. Many of the birds at the Zoo, such as cranes, stone curlews and eagles, are in danger of extinction. Their nesting is carefully monitored so that an egg can be removed if the temperature is not right, and a chick helped from the shell if it is having difficulty breaking out. There are about 350 kinds of birds at London Zoo.

Now go to the big-cat arena where you can see leopards, lions, tigers, jaguars and cheetahs. To the south of the cats, you will find a children's farm and, to the west, the penguins and seals. Don't miss seeing the penguins being fed at 2.30.

Next you can visit the rhinos and elephants. In January 1983, the Zoo began putting marmoset monkeys in with the elephants and rhinos. They are very inquisitive and you may find them getting close to you.

The next animals to visit are the storks, ostriches and sea lions. Then go into the reptile house where you will see cobras, pythons, vipers, and rattlesnakes.

In the Aquarium, there are Fresh and Sea Water Halls. In the Fresh Water Hall, you will find salmon whose parents spawned in the Thames River. The Thames is now considered to be one of the cleanest rivers in any capital city.

In the Sea Water Hall, you will see octopuses; they cannot use recycled sea water, only new. There is one who has a flower-pot home. Perhaps you will see a father sea-horse carrying his baby in a pouch on his stomach.

Leave the zoo at the front entrance and turn to the right. You will pass the offices of the Zoological Society of London on your left and an entrance into Regent's Park on your right.

Cross at the traffic lights and walk up Parkway to Camden High Street. Camden Underground will be on the opposite side of Camden High Street and to your left.

Did You Spot?
1. The bird with a long black beak, white body and black tail in the Snowdon Aviary?
2. Their nest? If so, what was it?
3. Which is the biggest ape?
4. What animal in the zoo is the ancestor of our domestic pig?

Do You Know?
5. The main food of the Panda bear?
6. Which areas elephants come from?
7. What the fastest cat is?
8. What insect other than ants an anteater eats?
9. What makes it possible for snakes to swallow their food whole?
10. Why frogs change colour?

Answers

Tour 1
1. Cock
2. I counted 14
3. Queen Anne, who was Queen when St Paul's was finished
4. Roundheads
5. Because his diaries tell us much about the Great Fire and the Plague
6. Prince Albert
7. Prince Charles and Princess Diana
8. Founder of the nursing profession
9. The Iron Duke

Tour 2
1. Uriah Heep
2. Gold beater's arm
3. Needlework
4. Races
5. *Pickwick Papers*
6. With a ladle or pan
7. It is made of sugar
8. 1500–1600
9. Duke of Wellington

Tour 3
1. An execution block
2. A dolphin and a girl
3. A lady
4. Ravens
5. Traitors' Gate
6. The Royal Zoo was kept in it until 1834
7. Sir Walter Raleigh
8. On the Queen's birthday, the birth of a Royal infant, and when the Queen opens Parliament in person
9. The Scavenger's Daughter
10. From rats which came on ships

Tour 4
1. Sentry Box
2.
3. Lion
4. Victory
5. A crown
6. Grenadier Guards
7.
8. It was very low

Tour 5
1. Beetles
2. Mulberry
3. Butterflies and a bird
4. Fossil
5. Neanderthal
6. Oil
7. Brain
8. Bustles
9. Stradivarius

Tour 6
1. 1754–1912
2. A girl, a ship and a basket of flowers
3. Harp
4. Wood
5. Germany
6. Wood, papier-maché, wax, bisque, porcelain, cloth, celluloid, plastic
7. Lead soldiers

8. Queen Mary
9. Rushes were dipped in fat
10. She stood in shop windows to advertise fashions being sold

Tour 7

1.
2. George Frederick Handel
3. A stagecoach
4. *Tom Brown's Schooldays*
5. 'Dr Livingstone, I presume?'
6. The Boy Scouts
7. Lord Horatio Nelson
8. Franklin Delano Roosevelt
9. Tobacco
10. Crusade

Tour 8

1. Charles Chaplin
2. Sebastion Coe
3. Florence Nightingale
4. The four people on the right were added later. They have Elizabethan clothes on
5. Queen Elizabeth and Princess Margaret
6. Queen Elizabeth I
7. The Bard
8. Physicist
9. Halley's Comet
10. It magnifies the paintings on the ceiling

Tour 9

1. 14
2. Lion
3. In a pocket
4. To Somerset House
5. A polar bear
6. Queen Anne, wife of James I
7. Henry VIII
8. On the ship *Victory*
9. To carry admirals to their ships
10. Explorer. He also discovered

how to prevent scurvy with a diet high in Vitamin C

Tour 10

1. Wooden tablets coated with beeswax
2. The Lord Mayor's Coach
3. Legionnaires
4. Julius Caesar
5. Oranges and Lemons
6. How to conduct lightning
7. Shakespeare
8. 51

Tour 11

1. To polish steel ornaments
2. 1813
3. Model N Ford
4. George Stephenson
5. Photographic negative
6. Periscope
7. Ruby or Garnet
8. Sulphur
9. Washing away of the soil
10. Lava

Tour 12

1. A cable attached to the river bed
2. 1939
3. The Blitz
4. To prevent flooding or gas entering the room
5. British Broadcasting Corporation
6. Security
7. Her (His) Majesty's Ship
8. Mrs Neville Chamberlain
9. Magnetic
10. D-Day

Tour 14

1. The Duke of Wellington
2. Hammocks
3. King Richard III
4. V – for Victory
5. The Roundheads
6. 'The Ugly Duckling'

7. Her pet dog
8. Mme DuBarry (1743–93), guillotined also
9. The United States of America
10. Lionheart

Tour 15
1. Foxhunt
2. Painter
3. China
4. Acorn
5. Scotland
6. American War of Independence
7. Furniture maker
8. York
9. *Pickwick Papers*

Tour 16
1. Messrs Fortnum and Mason came out
2. Morning suits
3. Christopher
4. King Henry VIII
5. Spider

Tour 17
1. Spurs
2. 4
3. Cat and eel
4. Snail
5. The Ambassadors
6. Music, arithmetic, geometry, astronomy
7. Skull
8. Twice. They are reflected in the mirror
9. Virginal
10. Horatio

Tour 18
1. Limewood
2. Will Somers
3. Cardinal Wolsey
4. King Charles Cavalier
5. Catherine of Aragon, Anne Boleyn, Jane Seymour, Anne of Cleves, Catherine Howard, Catherine Parr
6. In 1540
7. Oliver Cromwell
8. Queen Anne
9. King James I
10. Germany

Tour 19
1. Antarctica
2. Oliver Cromwell
3. Rosetta Stone
4. A fly
5. Jigsaw
6. Punch and Judy
7. King John
8. Coliseum
9. Turkey
10. About AD 600

Tour 20
1. Staghorn
2. 10
3. Captain Cook
4. Meat eater
5. Dye
6. Confectionery and textiles
7. Inner bark of shoots of the plant
8. The dried flower buds
9. China
10. A blacksmith

Tour 21
1. Cannon
2. Queen Victoria
3. Hat and scarf
4. 12
5. Clock
6. Diamond Jubilee (60 years)
7. Isambard Kingdom Brunel
8.
9. Dragon
10. 'The grand old Duke of York, he had ten thousand men. He marched them up to the top of the hill and he marched them down again.'

Tour 22
1. Sheep
2. Egyptian Service
3. A figure of Victory
4. Clay pipe and a tankard
5. Goya (Francisco de Goya y Lucientes, 1746–1828)
6. 26 feet
7. Marengo
8. Tiger skin
9. The Great Hall
10. Canada

Tour 23
1. 11
2. Sound locator
3.
4. Helping people find relatives after a bombing raid
5. 9 May 1940
6. The Montgolfier Brothers
7. 1785
8. He is a pilot making his escape
9. The rope-like circle above his head

Tour 26
1. The Duke of Wellington
2. A grasshopper
3. Winston Churchill
4. Prince Charles
5. Cat
6. Lady Jane Grey
7. 1 foot, 2 feet, 1 imperial yard, 1 metre
8. 2nd Century BC

9. Mary Queen of Scots
10. Hour glass

Tour 27
1. Telephone
2. 12
3. Door handle
4. Parrot
5. Hetty
6. Sam
7. Noble organ
8. A gout chair
9. That he be given his freedom (he was a slave)
10. The Garret (or attic)

Tour 29
1. 10
2. Whip
3. Covered in black
4. To prevent flying glass from injuring the passengers
5. Because it had high padded seats and small slit windows

Tour 30
1. Sacred Ibis
2. Willow tree
3. Gorilla, 180kg (400 lb)
4. Wild boar
5. Bamboo shoots
6. Asia and Africa
7. Cheetah, 104 km/h (64 mph)
8. Termites
9. The specially hinged jawbone
10. To camouflage themselves

Index

NOTES

NOTES

NOTES

NOTES

NOTES

Books of historical interest now available in
Panther Books

David Daiches
Edinburgh (illustrated)   £1.95 ☐
Glasgow (illustrated)   £2.50 ☐
Paul Johnson
The National Trust Book of British Castles (illustrated)   £3.95 ☐
Nigel Nicolson
The National Trust Book of Great Houses (illustrated)   £3.95 ☐
Frank Delaney
James Joyce's Odyssey (illustrated)   £2.95 ☐
Stan Gébler Davies
James Joyce: A Portrait of the Artist   £1.95p ☐
Peter Somerville-Large
Dublin (illustrated)   £2.25 ☐

To order direct from the publisher just tick the titles you want
and fill in the order form.   **GM681**

Titles of General Interest now available in Panther Books

Malcolm MacPherson (Editor)
The Black Box: Cockpit Voice Recorder
  Accounts of Nineteen Air Accidents £1.95 ☐

Isaac Asimov
Asimov on Science Fiction £2.50 ☐

Roy Harley Lewis
The Browser's Guide to Erotica £1.95 ☐

Charles Berlitz
Native Tongues £2.50 ☐

Carole Boyer
Names for Boys and Girls £1.25 ☐

José Silva and Michael Miele
The Silva Mind Control Method £2.50 ☐

Millard Arnold (editor)
The Testimony of Steve Biko £2.50 ☐

John Howard Griffin
Black Like Me £1.95 ☐

Desmond Morris
The Naked Ape £1.95 ☐
The Pocket Guide to Man Watching £2.95 ☐

Ivan Tyrell
The Survival Option £2.50 ☐

Peter Laurie
Beneath the City Streets £2.50 ☐

To order direct from the publisher just tick the titles you want
and fill in the order form.

Regional books in Panther Books

Showell Styles
Welsh Walks and Legends £1.00 ☐

Chris Barber
Mysterious Wales £2.50 ☐

Brian J. Bailey
Lakeland Walks and Legends £1.50 ☐

Robert Orrell
Saddle Tramp in the Lake District £1.50 ☐

Tom Weir
Weir's Way £2.50 ☐

David Daiches
Edinburgh £1.95 ☐
Glasgow £2.50 ☐

Peter Somerville-Large
Dublin £2.25 ☐

Frank Delaney
James Joyce's Odyssey £2.95 ☐

Mary Cathcart Borer
London Walks and Legends £1.95 ☐

Mary Peplow & Debra Shipley
London for Free £1.95 ☐

To order direct from the publisher just tick the titles you want
and fill in the order form.

HB1281

All these books are available at your local bookshop or newsagent, or can be ordered direct from the publisher.

To order direct from the publisher just tick the titles you want and fill in the form below.

Name ____

Address ____

____

Send to:
Panther Cash Sales
PO Box 11, Falmouth, Cornwall TR10 9EN.

Please enclose remittance to the value of the cover price plus:

UK 45p for the first book, 20p for the second book plus 14p per copy for each additional book ordered to a maximum charge of £1.63.

BFPO and Eire 45p for the first book, 20p for the second book plus 14p per copy for the next 7 books, thereafter 8p per book.

Overseas 75p for the first book and 21p for each additional book.

Panther Books reserve the right to show new retail prices on covers, which may differ from those previously advertised in the text or elsewhere.